History of United Arab Emirate

Travel and Tourism Information Guide

Author
David Mills.

SONITTEC PUBLISHING. All rights reserved. No part of this publication may be reproduced, distributed, or transmitted in any form or by any means, including photocopying, recording, or other electronic or mechanical methods, without the prior written permission of the publisher, except in the case of brief quotations embodied in critical reviews and certain other noncommercial uses permitted by copyright law. For permission requests, write to the publisher, addressed "Attention: Permissions Coordinator," at the address below.

Copyright © 2019 Sonittec Publishing
All Rights Reserved

First Printed: 2019.

Publisher:
SONITTEC LTD
College House, 2nd Floor
17 King Edwards Road,
Ruislip
London
HA4 7AE.

Table of Content

SUMMARY 1
INTRODUCTION 3
   Land 5
      Relief 6
      Drainage 6
      Climate 7
      Plant and animal life 7
PEOPLE 9
   Ethnic groups 9
   Languages and religion 9
   Settlement patterns and demographic trends 10
   Gastronomy 11
ECONOMY 13
   Agriculture and fishing 14
   Resources and power 15
   Manufacturing 17
   Finance 17
   Trade 18
   Services 19
   Labour and taxation 19
   Transportation and telecommunications 21
GOVERNMENT AND SOCIETY 23
   Constitutional framework 23
   Local government 24
   Justice 25
   Political process 25
   Security 26
   Health and welfare 26
   Housing 27
   Education 27
   Health & safety 28
CULTURAL LIFE 30
   Daily life and social customs 31
   The arts 33
   Cultural institutions 34
   Sports and recreation 34
   Media and publishing 34
HISTORY 36
   The struggle for centralization 37
   Foreign relations 39
EMIRATES 44
   Dubai 44

Dubai Culture	46
Sights in Dubai	50
Burj Al Arab	50
Al Bastakiya	51
Ferrari World	51
Saeed Al Maktoum House	52
Al Quoz	52
Jumeirah Beach	53
Dubai Heritage Village	54
The Dubai Fountain	54
Grand Mosque	55
Dubai Zoo	56
Dubai Butterfly Garden	56
Legoland Dubai	57
Aquaventure Waterpark	57
IMG Worlds of Adventures	58
Dubai Frame	59
Motiongate	59
Dubai Creek	60
Wild Wadi Water Park	61
Sharjah	62
Wadi Bih	62
Creek Park	62
Burj Khalifa	63
Children's City	64
The Lost Chambers Aquarium	64
Dubai Garden Glow	65
Dubai Miracle Garden	66
Dubai Festival City	66
ABU DHABI	67
Sights	71
Yas Island	71
St Andrew's Church	71
Al Wathba Wetland Reserve	72
Emirates National Auto Museum	72
Sheikh Zayed Grand Mosque	73
Masdar City	74
About Yas Waterworld	74
About Abu Dhabi Falcon Hospital	75
Eastern Mangrove Lagoon National Park	75
Corniche Beach	76
Observation Deck at 300	77
Yas Marina Circuit	77
Heritage Village	78
Zayed Heritage Center	79

- Delma Park 79
- Sheikh Zayed Cricket Stadium 80
- Kidoos Entertainment 80
- Etihad Modern Art Gallery 81
- Liwa Oasis 82
- Al Lulu Island 82
- Qasr Al-Hosn 83
- Aldar HQ Building 84
- St. Joseph's Cathedral 84
- Ferrari World 85
- Aldar HQ Building 85
- Mushrif Central Park 86
- Al Maqta'a Fort 86
- Green Mubazzarah 87
- Abu Dhabi Mar Thoma Church 88
- Murjan Splash Park 88
- MusicHall 89
- Al Bateen Beach 89
- Emirates Park Zoo 90
- Folklore Gallery 91
- Al Ain Zoo 91
- Emirates Palace 92
- Arabian Wildlife Park 92
- About Saadiyat Beach 93
- Manarat Al Saadiyat 94
- Sheikh Zayed Bridge 94
- Fun City 95
- Warehouse421 95

FUJAIRAH 96
- Sights 98
  - Al-Bidyah Mosque 98
  - Fujairah Fort 99
  - Ain al-Madhab Hot Springs 99
  - Fujairah Beaches 100
  - Masafi Market 100
  - Wadi Wurayah National Park 101
  - Sheikh Zayed Mosque 102
- Best Things to Do in Fujairah 103
- Diving and snorkelling: 103
- Where to eat 106
- What to see 108
- Where to stay 110

SHARJAH 112
- Cities/Towns 116
  - East Coast 116

- Khorfakkan ... 116
- Kalba ... 117
- Dibba ... 117
- Central Region ... 118
  - Al Dhaid ... 118
  - Al Badayer ... 119
- Traditions ... 119
  - National Men's Attire ... 120
  - National Women's Dress ... 120
  - Arabian Gulf Cuisine ... 121
  - Pastries & Sweets ... 122
  - Music, Dance & Folklore ... 122
  - Architecture ... 123
  - Dhows ... 124
  - Traditional Sports ... 124
- Culture ... 125
- Activities ... 132
  - Shopping ... 132
  - Entertainment ... 133
  - Sharjah Events ... 138
  - Beaches & Parks ... 145
  - Sports & Activities ... 150
  - Desert & Adventures ... 159
  - Culture & Heritage ... 160
  - Museums ... 165
  - Landmarks ... 174
  - Nature & Reserves ... 182

RAS AL KHAIMAH ... 187
- Attractions & nightlife ... 188
- Guide to Ras al Khaimah ... 191
- Culture: sights to visit ... 194

AJMAN ... 197
- Ajman Attraction ... 198
- Sightseeing ... 203
- Economy of Ajman ... 205
- Population of Ajman ... 206
- Major attractions in Ajman ... 206

UMM AL QUWAIN ... 209
- Attractions and Activities in Umm al Quwain ... 211
- Things to do in Umm Al Quwain ... 213

Summary

The world is a book and those who do not travel read only one page.

It is indeed very unfortunate that some people feel traveling is a sheer waste of time, energy and money. Some also find traveling an extremely boring activity. Nevertheless, a good majority of people across the world prefer traveling, rather than staying inside the confined spaces of their homes. They love to explore new places, meet new people, and see things that they would not find in their homelands. It is this very popular attitude that has made tourism, one of the most profitable, commercial sectors in the world.

People travel for various reasons. Some travel for work, others for fun, and some for finding mental peace. Though every person may have his/her own reason to go on a journey, it is essential to note that traveling, in itself, has some inherent advantages. For one, for some days getting away from everyday routine is a pleasant change. It not only refreshes one's body, but also mind and soul. Traveling to a distant place and doing exciting things that are not thought of otherwise, can rejuvenate a person, who then returns home, ready to take on new and more difficult challenges in life and work. It makes a person forget his worries, problems, frustrations, and fears, albeit for some time. It gives him a chance to think wisely and constructively. Traveling also helps to heal; it can mend a broken heart.

For many people, traveling is a way to attain knowledge, and perhaps, a quest to find answers to their questions. For this, many people prefer to go to faraway and isolated places. For believers, it is a search for God and to gain higher knowledge; for others, it is a search for inner peace. They might or might not find what they are looking for, but such an experience certainly enriches their lives

Introduction

United Arab Emirates is a federation of seven emirates along the eastern coast of the Arabian Peninsula.

The largest of these emirates, Abu Dhabi (Abū Ẓaby), which comprises more than three-fourths of the federation's total land area, is the centre of its oil industry and borders Saudi Arabia on the federation's southern and eastern borders. The port city of Dubai, located at the base of the mountainous Musandam Peninsula, is the capital of the emirate of Dubai (Dubayy) and is one of the region's most vital commercial and financial centres, housing hundreds of multinational corporations in a forest of skyscrapers. The smaller emirates of Sharjah (Al-Shāriqah), ʿAjmān, Umm al-Qaywayn, and Raʾs al-Khaymah also occupy the peninsula, whose protrusion north toward Iran forms the Strait of Hormuz linking the Persian Gulf to the Gulf of Oman. The federation's seventh member, Al-Fujayrah, faces the Gulf of Oman and is the only member of the union with no frontage along the Persian Gulf.

Historically the domain of individual Arab clans and families, the region now comprising the emirates also has been influenced by Persian culture owing to its close proximity to Iran, and its porous maritime borders have for centuries invited migrants and traders from elsewhere. In the 18th century, Portugal and the Netherlands extended their holdings in the region but retreated with the growth of British naval power there; following a series of truces with Britain in the 19th century, the emirates united to form the Trucial States (also called Trucial Oman or the Trucial Sheikhdoms). The states gained autonomy following World War II (1939–45), when the trucial states of Bahrain and Qatar declared independent statehood. The rest were formally united in 1971, with the city of Abu Dhabi serving as the capital. The stability of the federation has since been tested by rivalries between the families governing the larger states of Abu Dhabi and Dubai, though external events such as the Persian Gulf War (1990–91) and an ongoing territorial dispute with Iran have served to strengthen the emirates' political cohesion.

The emirates comprise a mixed environment of rocky desert, coastal plains and wetlands, and waterless mountains. The seashore is a haven for migratory waterfowl and draws birdwatchers from all over the world; the country's unspoiled beaches and opulent resorts also have drawn international travelers. Standing at a historic and geographic crossroads and made up of diverse nationalities and ethnic groups, the United Arab Emirates present a striking blend of ancient customs and modern technology, of cosmopolitanism and insularity, and of wealth and want. The rapid pace of modernization of the emirates prompted travel writer Jonathan Raban to note of the capital: "The condition of Abu Dhabi was so evidently mint that it would not have been surprising to see adhering to the buildings bits of straw and polystyrene from the crates in which they had been packed."

Land

The United Arab Emirates is slightly smaller in area than Portugal. It is bordered by Saudi Arabia to the west and south and by Oman to the east and northeast. The precise borders of the country have remained a matter of dispute. Despite a 1974 secret agreement between the United Arab Emirates and Saudi Arabia said to have resolved their three border disputes, the agreement's legal standing is unclear. The United Arab Emirates claims a strip of coastline that borders Qatar to the northwest, which Saudi Arabia claims was ceded to it in the 1974 agreement. It likewise disputes Saudi claims over the Shaybah oil field to the south, while Saudi Arabia (as well as Oman) has at times challenged the emirates' claim on oases around the city of Al-'Ayn. Since the early 1990s, moreover, the emirates have been in a dispute with Iran over the ownership of three islands Abū Mūsā and Greater and Lesser Tunb (Ṭunb al-Kubrā and Ṭunb al-Ṣughrā).

Relief

Nearly the entire country is desert, containing broad areas of sand. Some of the world's largest sand dunes are located east of ʿArādah in the oases of Al-Liwāʾ. Important oases are at Al-ʿAyn about 100 miles (160 km) east of Abu Dhabi. Along the eastern portion of the Musandam Peninsula, the northern extension of the Ḥajar Mountains (also shared by Oman) offers the only other major relief feature; elevations rise to about 6,500 feet (2,000 metres) at their highest point. The Persian Gulf coast is broken by shoals and dotted with islands that offer shelter to small vessels. There are, however, no natural deepwater harbours; both Dubai's Port Rāshid and the gigantic Port Jebel Ali, 20 miles (32 km) southwest of Dubai city, are man-made, as are major ports in Abu Dhabi, Sharjah, and Raʾs al-Khaymah. The coast of the Gulf of Oman is more regular and has three natural harbours Dibā, Khawr Fakkān, and Kalbā.

Drainage

The United Arab Emirates has no perennial streams nor any regularly occurring bodies of surface water. Precipitation, what little falls, is drained from the mountains in the form of seasonal wadis that terminate in inland salt flats, or *sabkhah*s, whose drainage is frequently blocked by the country's constantly shifting dunes. In the far west the Maṭṭī Salt Flat extends southward into Saudi Arabia, and coastal *sabkhah*s, which are occasionally inundated by the waters of the Persian Gulf, lie in the areas around Abu Dhabi.

Climate

The climate is hot and humid along the coast and is hotter still, but dry, in the interior. Rainfall averages only 4 to 6 inches (100 to 150 mm) annually, though it fluctuates considerably from year to year. The average January temperature is 64 °F (18 °C), while in July the temperature averages 91 °F (33 °C). Summertime highs can reach 115 °F (46 °C) on the coast and 120 °F (49 °C) or more in the desert. In midwinter and early summer, winds known as the *shamāl* (Arabic: "norther") blow from the north and northwest, bearing dust and sand.

Plant and animal life

Because of the desert climate, vegetation is scanty and largely limited to the low shrubs that offer forage to nomadic herds, but millions of trees, notably mangroves, have been planted in Abu Dhabi and have provided habitats for various species. In the oases, date palms are raised together with alfalfa (lucerne). Fruits are grown, and the Al-'Ayn oases east of Abu Dhabi are known for their mangoes. Animal life includes domesticated goats, sheep, and camels, together with cattle and poultry, which were introduced in more recent times. Wildlife consists of predators such as the caracal, sand cat (*Felis margarita*), and the Ruppell's (*Vulpes ruppelli*) and red foxes; larger animals such as the Arabian oryx and Arabian and Persian gazelles; smaller mammals such as the cape hare, lesser jerboa, and various types of gerbil; and a variety of snakes and lizards. The gulf waters harbour schools of mackerel, grouper, tuna, and porgies, as well as sharks and occasional whales. In the 1990s the government initiated a conservation and management program to preserve and protect desert animal and plant life.

People

Ethnic groups

Only about one-eighth of the emirates' residents are citizens. The remainder are mostly foreign workers and their dependents, with South Asians constituting the largest of these groups. Arabs from countries other than the United Arab Emirates and Iranians account for another significant portion. Southeast Asians, including many Filipinos, have immigrated in increasing numbers to work in various capacities.

Languages and religion

The official language of the United Arab Emirates is Standard Arabic. Nonetheless, English is also spoken in the country. The English language is mostly used in business relations and in educating the students of the country. Together with Arabic, English is a great combination of communicating especially with the foreign traders and businessmen and other economic relations in the UAE. Medium of instructions in Arabic and English are emphasized in public and private schools.

The Standard Arabic is a combination from Afro-Asiatic, Semitic, and Central and Southern Arabic. The Standard Arabic, also known as the Literary Arabic, is focused and used in writing and in speech as well. According to the scholars, the Arabic language is comprised of two kinds: the Classic Arabic and the Modern Standard Arabic. Books, magazines, and newspapers in the country are using the Modern Standard Arabic. Moreover, the Modern Standard Arabic is primarily based on the Classic Arabic. Another kind of Arabic spoken in the country is the Gulf Spoken Arabic or the Gulf Arabic or the Khaliji, a language also spoken in various Persian Gulf nations (Kuwait, Saudi Arabia, Qatar, and Bahrain). Another of its variation is the Shihhi Arabic, a language mostly spoken in the Musandam Peninsula of Oman.

Other major languages in the UAE are Urdu, Hindi and Farsi. Several languages such as Persian, Balochi, Hindi, Urdu, Tamil, Malayalam, Pashto, Bengali and Tagalog are also spoken by the numerous expatriates in the country from South East Asia, Africa, and Indian sub-continents.

Settlement patterns and demographic trends

The population of the United Arab Emirates is concentrated primarily in cities along both coasts, although the interior oasis settlement of Al-'Ayn has grown into a major population centre as well. Several emirates have exclaves within other emirates.

The federation's birth rate is one of the lowest among the Persian Gulf states, and the infant mortality rate has decreased substantially. Owing to the large number of foreign workers, more than two-thirds of the population is male. The country's death rate is well below the world average, and the average life expectancy is about 78 years. The major causes of death are cardiovascular disease, accidents and poisonings, and cancer.

Gastronomy

Never leave the borders beyond the country without filling your stomach with wondrous food of the Emiratis. A blend in style of diverse cultures inhabiting the country provides the palate a unique satisfaction in several ways that a mouth craves for every minute. Be dazzled with every combination of Middle East, Asian cuisine, and food rooted from the Arabic heritage. Flavours that enhance the taste buds' preference will have your tummy relaxed and fulfilled in the country's dishes and menus. The Emirati cookery introduces a realm of meat, dairy, spices, and sweets to everyone's food desires. Some traditional dishes in the country include Fireed, Jisheid, and Mishwy to be enjoyed with. Camel meat is also indulged but usually in special occasions.

Arab menus do not include pork because most of the inhabitants of the country are Muslims and they are prohibited to eat such. Beef, lamb, fish, and rice are commonly eaten in the country. Beverages such as coffee and tea with other flavour-adding ingredients such as saffron and mint increase the drinks' tastefulness. One of the most popular cuisines of the country is the Arabic Mezze, usually eaten by the hand, a combination of chicken shawarma and a bread to scoop it. Another sophisticated dish of the country that is a must-try is a delectable Kebab Kashkash, a serve of meat and spices in a flavoursome tomato sauce. On the other hand, international cuisines are also plentiful in the country. Spicy rice dishes of the Iranians and the Arabic bread, fresh salad, and pickles combinations by the Lebanese are also remarkable to the country's numerous cuisines.

Economy

The economic development of the United Arab Emirates has rapidly advanced because of abundant resources in the country. Export goods such as crude oil, natural gas, and dates have been copious and have greatly benefited the country's economic factors. The United Arab Emirates is a member of the World Trade Organization, with boosting construction projects expanding the country's flourishing service sector. Around $270 billion dollars in 2008 is the estimated GDP of the country, bringing it third in the Middle East and in the 38th position in the world.

The wealthiest emirate of the country is the Abu Dhabi, which is controlled by the Abu Dhabi Investment Authority. Imports in the country are also valuable with increasing manufacture of goods. Numerous power plants and industries also play an important role in the growth of the country's economy. The country is a member of the Gulf Cooperation Council which focuses on economic issues such as developing common policies in trade, finance, transportation, and individual economic rights.

Although the country is abundant with oil, it has developed a non-independent to oil GDP; with other sources of revenue such as tourism and finance sectors. The country has gradually improved and widely promoted high-class tourism endeavours enriching the country's significant places and tourist spots. The Dubai International Financial Centre is advantageous for it offers 55.5% of foreign ownership with no withholding tax, with tailor-made financial system. The liberalisation in the country's property market has gained many investors and has increased the country's boom in real estate sectors

Agriculture and fishing

Agricultural production centred largely in the emirates of Ra's al-Khaymah and Al-Fujayrah, in the two exclaves of ʿAjmān, and at Al-ʿAyn has expanded considerably through the increased use of wells and pumps to provide water for irrigation. However, agriculture contributes only a small fraction of gross domestic product (GDP) and employs less than one-tenth of the workforce. Dates are a major crop, as are tomatoes, cucumbers, and eggplants, and the United Arab Emirates is nearly self-sufficient in fruit and vegetable production. The country also produces enough eggs, poultry, fish, and dairy products to meet its own needs but must import most other foodstuffs, notably grains. The Arid Lands Research Centre at Al-ʿAyn experiments with raising crops in a desert environment. Most commercial fishing is concentrated in Umm al-Qaywayn, and the emirates have one of the largest fishing sectors in the Arab world.

Resources and power

Oil was discovered in Abu Dhabi in 1958, and the government of that emirate owns a controlling interest in all oil-producing companies in the federation through the Abu Dhabi National Oil Company (ADNOC). Abu Dhabi is responsible for about 95 percent of the country's oil production, and production of petroleum and natural gas contributes about one-third of the nation's GDP, even though the oil and gas sector employs only a tiny fraction of the workforce. The largest petroleum concessions are held by an ADNOC subsidiary, Abu Dhabi Marine Operating Company (ADMA-OPCO), which is partially owned by British, French, and Japanese interests. One of the main offshore fields is located in Umm al-Shā'if. Al-Bunduq offshore field is shared with neighbouring Qatar but is operated by ADMA-OPCO. A Japanese consortium operates an offshore rig at Al-Mubarraz, and other offshore concessions are held by American companies. Onshore oil concessions are held by another ADNOC company, the Abu Dhabi Company for Onshore Oil Operations, which is likewise partially owned by American, French, Japanese, and British interests. Other concessions also are held by Japanese companies.

Petroleum production in Dubai began in 1969. There are offshore oil fields at Ḥaql Fatḥ, Fallah, and Rāshid. The emirate long maintained a controlling interest in its oil fields and took full control of oil production in 2007. At its peak, Dubai produced about one-sixth of the country's total output of petroleum. Production dwindled to a negligible amount, however, as the emirate diversified its economy. Sharjah began producing oil in 1974; another field, predominantly yielding natural gas, was discovered six years later. In 1984 oil production began off the shore of Ra's al-Khaymah, in the Persian Gulf.

The federation's natural gas reserves are among the world's largest, and most fields are found in Abu Dhabi. In the late 1990s the United Arab Emirates began investing heavily to develop its natural gas sector, both for export and to fire domestic thermal power plants.

Because it relies on energy-intensive technologies such as water desalination and air-conditioning and because subsidies on fuel have encouraged wasteful energy use, the United Arab Emirates has one of the world's highest per capita rates of energy consumption. Despite its large hydrocarbon reserves, rapidly increasing domestic demand driven by population growth and industrialization in the first decade of the 21st century forced the emirates to import natural gas and to draw upon petroleum reserves at a fraction of the export price.

To safeguard future hydrocarbon production, the federation began to explore other sources for domestic energy. In 2009 the emirates contracted the Korean Electric Power Company to build four nuclear reactors in the country by 2020. Abu Dhabi and Dubai also began to invest in renewable energy. In 2013 Abu Dhabi opened what, at the time, was one of the world's largest solar power plants, a 100-megawatt facility capable of powering up to 20,000 homes.

Manufacturing

The emirates have attempted to diversify their economy to avoid complete dependence on oil, and manufacturing has played a significant part in that effort. A petrochemicalindustrial complex has been established at Al-Ruways, 140 miles (225 km) southwest of Abu Dhabi city, with a petroleum refinery, a gas fractionation plant, and an ammonia and urea plant. Dubai's revenues have been invested in projects such as a dry dock and a trade centre; its first airport was expanded in the 2000s, while a second airport was built near the port of Jebel Ali, and additional hotels have been built, including the striking Burj al-'Arab ("Tower of the Arabs"), which opened in the late 1990s. The Burj Khalifa("Khalifa Tower") skyscraper in Dubai city became the world's tallest building and the tallest freestanding structure when it opened in 2010. Sharjah has built a cement plant, a plastic-pipe factory, and paint factories. Manufacturing accounts for less than one-tenth of GDP in the country overall.

Finance

The Central Bank of the United Arab Emirates was established in 1980, with Dubai and Abu Dhabi each depositing half of their revenues in the institution. The bank also issues the UAE dirham, the emirates' national currency. There are commercial, investment, development, foreign, and domestic banks as well as a bankers' association. In 1991 the worldwide operations of Abu Dhabi's Bank of Credit and Commerce International (BCCI), partly owned by the ruling family, were closed down after corrupt practices were uncovered, and the emirate subsequently created the Abu Dhabi Free Zone Authority to develop a new financial centre. The emirates' first official stock exchange, the Dubai Financial Market (Sūq Dubayy al-Mālī), was opened in 2000, followed by the Dubai International Financial Exchange in 2005.

Finance is an important component of the emirates' economy, and the country's liberal banking regulations have made it a popular destination for foreign funds, both open and clandestine. Dubai in particular has become a major world banking centre and a hub for unofficial financial institutions known as *ḥawālah*s (or *hundī*s), which specialize in transferring money internationally beyond state regulation. While such institutions are used primarily to transfer remittances, they also have been a way for terrorist organizations and criminal groups to move and launder illicit funds.

Trade

Trade has long been important to Dubai and Sharjah. Even before the discovery of oil, Dubai's prosperity was assured by its role as the

Persian Gulf's leading entrepôt. (It was known especially as a route for smuggling gold into India.) In 1995 the United Arab Emirates joined the World Trade Organization and since then has developed a number of free-trade zones, technology parks, and modern ports in order to attract trade. The large free-trade zone of Port Jebel Ali was developed during the 1980s and has done much to attract foreign manufacturing industries interested in producing goods for export.

Exports are dominated by petroleum and natural gas. Imports consist primarily of machinery and transport equipment, gold, precious stones, and foods. Major trading partners include China, India, Japan, western European countries, and South Korea. A large amount of trade is in reexports to neighbouring gulf countries.

Services

The service sector, including public administration, defense, tourism, and construction, has played an increasing role in the economy since the late 1990s, especially as the country attempted to attract tourists and foreign businesses. In order to develop its tourism and business sectors, the government has encouraged major infrastructure projects, especially construction of accommodation and transportation systems hotels, resorts, restaurants, and airport expansion.

Labour and taxation

Expatriate workers constitute about nine-tenths of the labour force, and more in some private sector areas. Conditions for these workers often can be harsh, and at the beginning of the 21st century, the state did not allow workers to organize. Like other gulf states that depend heavily on foreign workers, the emirates have attempted to reduce the number of foreign employees in a program known as Emiratization by providing incentives for businesses to hire Emirati nationals.

In the early 21st century the expatriate labour issue persisted despite landmark developments. New laws were instituted that ban work during the heat of the midday hours in summer and that prohibit the use of children (largely expatriate) as jockeys in camel races. In addition, a number of strikes and protests in 2005 by unpaid expatriate labourers against a major construction and development company were resolved in favour of the workers. Early in 2006 the government announced the drafting of a new law permitting the formation of unions and wage bargaining; later that year, however, it instead passed a law permitting the deportation of striking workers, and worker organization remained illegal. The government gradually granted additional protections and rights to workers over the years, though it was not until 2017 that the United Arab Emirates' labour laws met the minimum standards of the International Labour Organization.

There is no income tax in the United Arab Emirates, and corporate taxes are only levied on oil companies and foreign banks. The bulk of government revenue is generated from nontax incomes, largely from the sale of petroleum products, but the government has begun supplementing its revenue with consumption taxes. An excise tax on carbonated beverages, energy drinks, and tobacco products was implemented in 2017. In 2018 the United Arab Emirates, in coordination with other gulf countries, implemented a value-added tax for most goods and services.

Transportation and telecommunications

An excellent road system, developed in the late 1960s and '70s, carries motor vehicles throughout the country and links it to its neighbours. The addition of a tunnel to the bridges connecting Dubai city and the nearby commercial centre of Dayrah facilitates the movement of traffic across the small saltwater inlet that separates them. The cities of Abu Dhabi, Dubai, Sharjah, Ra's al-Khaymah, Al-Fujayrah, and Al-'Ayn are served by international airports. A second airport opened to service Dubai in 2010. The older airport at Dubai is one of the busiest in the Middle East. The federation has a number of large and modern seaports, including the facilities at Dubai's Port Rāshid, which is serviced by a vast shipyard, and Port Jebel Ali, situated in one of the largest man-made harbours in the world and one of the busiest ports in the gulf. Of the smaller harbours on the Gulf of Oman, Sharjah has a modest port north of the city. In September 2009 the first portion of a remote-controlled rapid-transit metro line the gulf region's first metro system began operations in Dubai. Additional public transit projects, including monorail service in Abu Dhabi and linkages to the Saudi rail networks, have been planned as well. A Hyperloop system is likewise planned to connect Abu Dhabi and Dubai.

The state-controlled Emirates Telecommunications Corporation, known as Etisalat (Ittiṣālāt), is a major telecommunications provider in the country. Radio, television, telephone, and cellular telephone service is prevalent and widely used. In 2000 Etisalat began providing Internet service, and the emirates soon had one of the largest subscriber bases per capita in the Middle East. In 2005 a second licensed operator, Emirates Integrated Telecommunications Company (du), began providing telephone and high-speed Internet service, and in 2006 they reached an agreement with Etisalat to link their networks.

Government and Society

Constitutional framework

The Government of the United Arab Emirates is Federal Constitutional Monarchy. Seven absolute monarchies comprise the country's federation and are divided into emirates Abu Dhabi, Ajman, Dubai, Fujairah, Sharjah, Ras al-Khaimah, and Uhm al-Qwain. The head of the state is the President, and the head of the government is the Prime Minister of the United Arab Emirates. Moreover, concerns in foreign affairs, labour relations, banking, communications services, education, health, defense, security, nationality and immigration issues, economic issues, traffic control, delimitations of territorial waters, aircraft licensing, and extradition of criminals are also responsibilities of the Prime Minister of the country. Executive, legislative, and judiciary are the branches of the United Arab Emirates' government.

The executive branch of the government includes the President, Vice President, Prime Minister, Federal Supreme Council, and a Council of Ministers. Furthermore, the Federal Supreme Council of the country comprises of the emirs (generals) of the seven emirates. The council elects the president, vice president, the members of the Council of Ministers, and the judges of the Federal Supreme Council itself. The Supreme Council is the one responsible for formulating government policies, laws, and treatises. The president and the vice president of the country are hereditary; with the emir of the Abu Dhabi as the president and the emir of Dubai as the prime minister. A federal court system is applied to all seven emirates except Dubai and Ras Al Khaimah.

Liberal laws with civil law jurisdiction are practiced in the country. Yet, Shari'a Law or the Islamic Law is applied to family law, inheritance, and other criminal acts

Local government

The United Arab Emirates has a federal system of government, and any powers not assigned to the federal government by the constitution devolve to the constituentemirates. Generally, the distribution of power within the federal system is similar to those in other such systems for example, the federation government administers foreign policy, determines broad economic policy, and runs the social welfare system and a significant amount of power is exercised at the individual emirate level, notably in Abu Dhabi and Dubai.

Justice

The constitution calls for a legal code based on Sharī'ah (Islamic law). In practice, the judiciary blends Western and Islamic legal principles. At the federal level the judicial branch consists of the Union Supreme Court and several courts of first instance: the former deals with emirate-federal or inter-emirate disputes and crimes against the state, and the latter cover administrative, commercial, and civil disputes between individuals and the federal government. Other legal matters are left to local judicial bodies.

Political process

On the whole, leadership in each emirate falls to that emirate's most politically prominent tribe (an agnatic lineage group composed of a number of related families), and the paramount leader, the emir, is selected by the notables of the ruling tribe from among their number this is usually, but not always, a son of the previous emir. Each tribe, however, has its own leader, or sheikh, and a certain degree of political pluralism is necessary to maintain the ruling family's position. This is largely facilitated by the institution called the *majlis*, the council meeting. During the *majlis* the leader hears grievances, mediates disputes, and disperses largesse, and, in theory, anyone under the leader's rule must be granted access to the *majlis*.

Until the beginning of the 21st century, there were no political parties in the emirates, and no elections were held. Since 2006 an electoral college has met every several years to select half of the membership of the advisory Federal National Council; the other half is designated by appointment. In 2006 the electoral college consisted of fewer than 7,000 citizens, but it expanded in subsequent elections. By 2015, when the third election was held, the electoral college included more than 224,000, about one-third of voting-age citizens.

Security

The emirates' defense forces were merged in 1976, but the forces in Dubai and Abu Dhabihave retained some independence. The Supreme Council has made the right to raise armed forces a power of the national government. In 2006 the Supreme National Security Council, which included the president, prime minister, and chief of staff of the armed forces, among others, was formed to deal with the emirates' security needs. The number of uniformed military personnel is high for a country the size of the emirates, as is total military spending per capita. Most personnel are in the army, but the emirates maintain a small navy and air force, and a large number of expatriates serve in the military.

Health and welfare

Hospital services are free to nationals, and medical services are concentrated in Dubai and Abu Dhabi, which have numerous hospitals, child welfare clinics, and other health facilities. In the late 1990s the emirates began privatizing health care, which led to a significant rise in the number of hospitals and physicians. Government spending on health care has also increased.

Housing

A considerable proportion of government spending, at both the federal and local levels, is devoted to constructing and financing housing and to developing civil infrastructuresuch as power, water, and waste removal. The federation government makes housing available to citizens through direct low-interest loans, subsidies on rental units, and grants of housing at no charge, and thousands of Emiratis have taken advantage of these programs.

Education

The educational sector of the United Arab Emirates has been invested to provide quality, comprehensive education for all males and females from primary level to university level. Citizens of the country are provided with free education in government schools and universities. Private education sector is also offered in the country, with enormous school to be chosen from. The student populations of the country have pursued courses outside the country, mostly supported by the government. Progress of the literacy rates in the country have been increasing, with the government's approximately 25% allotment of budget to the country's education. The country's literacy rate is around 91%, with its system's efficiency applied to the citizens of the country for their greater benefit has the goal to achieve its fullest around the year 2010.

Eradicating illiteracy has been one of the programs in the country to greatly improve its people, with certain associations like the UAE Women's Federation focusing among the older members of the society to be educated. Moreover, greater opportunities have been offered in the country; the youth having the access to formal education, higher education, and free education to all men and women funded federally. Educational grants have also been offered. Furthermore, the educational development of the country has progressed through strategies, policies, and greater investments for the educational sector. By also equipping the students to have further future in the country's workforce, the people have been able to raise the country's development and have widely been educated with modern technology and other continuous education programs.

Health & safety

Focus on health care has been one of the topmost priorities of the country. Aiming to develop and improve materials and people facilities, the country has utmost provided government-funded health service and private health sector service as well. Government investment to the health sector has made the country efficient in facilitating healthcare among its people. Ranking 43rd among 174 developing countries in the UN Human Development Report, the country has greatly focused on the welfare and care of its inhabitants. Life expectancy rate is 74 years for men and 76 years for women. Child mortality rates are around 9 per 1000.

Eradication of illnesses has been made offering specialized services especially in public hospitals. Moreover, the country's public hospitals also provide state-of-the-art facilities and the health care infrastructures are also improved regularly. Progress in health care has emerged in the country, with the government allotting 81% of its budget to this sector. With this the United Arab Emirates is also listed as the fourth most developed Arab state in the Human Development Index (HDI), measure the overall achievements in a country in basic areas of human development such as life expectancy, education, and general standard of living. Developments in the country's healthcare are rapidly enhancing the way of living in the United Arab Emirates.

Preventive medicines are also the major concerns of the country. Widening immunization, public awareness, research, and educational programmes are implemented in the established nine preventive medicine centres in the country.

Cultural Life

Diverse culture emanates in the United Arab Emirates. Once a homogeneous country, the country had then been filled with different ethnic compositions and people from other countries. The Emirati culture is traced from the nomadic Bedouins, the desert culture, Arab culture, and the sea-oriented culture. The first settlers and influential people of the country were the Iranians followed by the Pakistanis and the Indians. The Emirati culture is centered in Islamic United Arab Emirates culture. Majority of the country's occupants are Muslims and the rest are Christians, Hindus, Buddhists, Sikhs, and Persis. The country has carefully preserved the country's culture and heritage, with Abu Dhabi Cultural Foundation heading to the United Arab Emirates' enrichment of art.

Eid al Fitr, marking the end of Ramadan; and the National Day, remembering the country's formation are significant events celebrated in the country. Manners and etiquette are strictly observed in the country ranging from dress codes to behaviours.

The Emirati literature varies from different forms and styles of poetry of patriotism, chivalry, religion, love, and family. One of the remarkable poets of the United Arab Emirates is Ibn Majid, composing 40 poems. Museums have also been abundant in the country, especially in the Sharjah region, having a total of 17 museums; which was hailed in 1998 the Cultural Capital of the Arab World. Foreign and indigenous art have been the highlights of the country's art preservation. Moreover, the country's music is rooted in Bedouin folk music, a music that has been passed from generation to generation and has been used in the country for many decades

Daily life and social customs

In several ways, change is apparent in the federation's cultural life. Changes in attitudes toward marriage and the employment of women are discernible. Some women are now given more choice in a marriage partner, and they have gained greater access to education and some types of professional work. New forms of entertainment, ranging from football (soccer) matches to DVD players, have affected taste and behaviour.

Although few Emiratis retain the lifeways of their forebears practicing a nomadic lifestyle or plying the Persian Gulf in search of fish and pearls many traditional modes of living continue. The major Islamic holidays, including the two ʿīds (festivals), ʿĪd al-Fiṭr and ʿĪd al-Aḍḥā, are observed among the Muslim majority, and traditional dress is still the norm. For women, traditional attire consists of a light chemise known as a *dir'*, which is often worn beneath a more ornate dress (*thawb*). Beneath the dress a *sirwāl*, a type of loose trouser, is worn. Outside the home or in the presence of strangers, women still cover themselves with a dark cloak known as an *'abāyah* and cover their heads with a scarf called a *shāl*, which may also serve as a veil (*ḥijāb* or *burqu'*). Fabrics are often delicate, colourful, and highly embroidered, and Emirati women wear a variety of fine gold and silver jewelry.

The traditional garb for men consists of a long, simple, ankle-length garment known as a *dishdashah* (or *thawb*). Usually made of white cotton, the *dishdashah* may also be of a heavier material and may be made in a variety of colours. The standard head covering is the *ghuṭrah*, a light scarf (usually white or white and red checkered, also known as a kaffiyeh) held in place by a black cord of camel hair known as an *'iqāl*. Colour, style, and material of head-wear may vary among groups.

Emirati cuisine reflects the variety of cultural influences that the country has experienced over the centuries. Hummus, *fūl* (spiced bean paste), falafel, and shawarma (broiled meat served on flat bread) are dishes standard to the Arab world, whereas the influence of Iranian cuisine can be seen in the Emirati preference for rice as a staple and ingredients such as saffron, cardamom, and rose water as flavouring in desserts. As in all countries of the region, lamb and chicken are the preferred meats, and fresh fruits including dates, figs, lemons, and limes vegetables, and unleavened bread (*khubz*) are daily fare. The preferred drink is coffee, served in the popular fashion hot, strong, and sweet.

The arts

As is true of other countries of the Arabian Peninsula, traditional arts such as pottery, weaving, and metalworking occupy a prominent place in cultural life. The manufacture of handicrafts is an economic mainstay for smaller villages, providing goods to sell in the souks (open-air markets) that lie at the heart of small towns and large cities alike. Traditional storytelling remains a much-admired art form, and Emirati culture, like Arab culture on the whole, esteems poetry, whether it is classical, contemporary, or the Bedouin vernacular form called *nabaṭī*. Traditional music, such as the *ḥudā'* sung originally by caravanners while on the trail is enjoyed alongside popular music from abroad, and traditional dances such as the *'ayyālah* (often called *'arḍah*), a type of sword dance, are performed on special occasions.

The Ministry of Information and Culture sponsors a number of events annually, including plays and music festivals, and helps support the numerous folklore associations in the emirates. The Sharjah Theatre Festival brings together talent from all seven emirates. Annual international book fairs in Sharjah and Abu Dhabi cities are highly regarded, and film festivals in the emirates are gaining in popularity and reputation. The Dubai Air Show has become a major regional event.

Cultural institutions

Dubai Museum is located in al-Fahīdī Fort and features displays on Bedouin life, local history, dances, and musical instruments. The fort is also home to a military museum. Al-'Ayn is the site of a museum devoted to Bedouin culture and the emirates' pre-oil history. Sharjah city features a noted natural history museum. Dubai city is growing as a centre for regional film, television, and music production.

Sports and recreation

Sports are popular in the United Arab Emirates and are strongly supported by the government. The Ministry of Youth and Sports oversees and encourages the many groups, clubs, and associations that provide sports-related activities. Football (soccer) is the most-watched spectator sport, and horse racing also enjoys widespread popularity. The federation is also a major centre for camel racing, a traditional sport that became increasingly popular late in the 20th century, and for falconry, once an important means of hunting. Dubai hosts many international sporting events, most notably for golf, tennis, rugby, and boat racing. The country made its Olympic debut at the 1984 Summer Games.

Media and publishing

The news media are concentrated in Abu Dhabi, Dubai, and Sharjah. A number of daily newspapers are published, in both Arabic and English. Radio and television programs are broadcast daily from Abu Dhabi, Dubai, Sharjah, and Ra's al-Khaymah, in those same languages.

History

This discussion focuses on the United Arab Emirates since the 19th century. For a treatment of earlier periods and of the country in its regional context, *see* Arabia, history of.

In the late 18th and early 19th centuries, the dominant tribal faction was the Qasimi family (Āl Qawāsim; singular Qāsimī), whose ships controlled the maritime commerce (notably fishing and pearling) concentrated in the lower Persian Gulf and in much of the Indian Ocean. Attacks on British and Indian ships led to a British naval attack in 1819 that defeated the Qasimi forces, and the British became dominant in the region.

The Qasimi family thus lost power and influence in the region, and the Banū Yās tribal confederation of Abu Dhabi became dominant. The Banū Yās were centred on the Al-ʿAyn and Al-Liwā' oases of Abu Dhabi, and their strength was land-based. Under the leadership of the Āl Nahyān (members of the Āl Bū Falāḥ tribe), the Banū Yās have been the most powerful element in the region since the mid-19th century.

The principal sheikhs along the coast signed a series of agreements during that century a general treaty of peace in 1820, the perpetual maritime truce in 1853 (which gave the Trucial Coast its name), and exclusive agreements in 1892 restricting their foreign relations to British discretion and the sheikhdoms became known as the Trucial States.

A council of the Trucial States began to meet semiannually in 1952 to discuss administrative issues. In January 1968, following the announcement by the British government that its forces would be withdrawn from the Persian Gulf by late 1971, Trucial Oman and the sheikhdoms of Qatar and Bahrain initiated plans to form a confederation. After three years of negotiations, however, Qatar and Bahrain decided to become independent sovereign states, and the former Trucial States, excluding Ra's al-Khaymah, announced the formation of the United Arab Emirates in December 1971. Ra's al-Khaymah joined the federation in February 1972.

The struggle for centralization

Abu Dhabi initiated a movement toward centralization in December 1973, when several of its former cabinet members took positions with the federal government. In May 1976 the seven emirates agreed to merge their armed forces, and in November of that year a provision was added to the constitution that gave the federal government the right to form an army and purchase weapons. Conflicts regarding centralization within the government in 1978 prompted Dubai and Ra's al-Khaymah to refuse to submit their forces to federal command, and Dubai began purchasing weapons independently. A proposal to form a federal budget, merge revenues, and eliminate internal boundaries was rejected by Dubai and Ra's al-Khaymah, in spite of strong domestic support. Dubai ended its opposition, however, when its ruler, Sheikh Rāshid ibn Saʿīd al-Maktūm, was offered the premiership of the federal government; he took office in July 1979. Sheikh Zāyid ibn Sulṭān al-Nahyān of Abu Dhabi served as president of the United Arab Emirates from 1971 to his death in 2004, when he was succeeded by his son Sheikh Khalifa ibn Zāyid al-Nahyān as ruler of Abu Dhabi and president of the emirates. Sheikh Rāshid of Dubai died in 1990, and his positions as ruler of Dubai and vice president and prime minister of the United Arab Emirates were assumed, successively, by his sons Sheikh Maktūm ibn Rāshid al-Maktūm (1990–2006) and, since 2006, Sheikh Muhammad ibn Rāshid al-Maktūm.

In 2006 the United Arab Emirates held its first elections. A very limited electoral collegewas permitted to vote for the selection of half of the membership of the advisory Federal National Council, the other half of which would remain designated by appointment.

The booming economy of the United Arab Emirates was slowed by the onset of the global financial crisis that began in 2008. The impact of the crisis was felt most in Dubai, where a number of large construction projects were suspended and real estate values dropped by 50 percent in a year. In late 2009 the government-run investment company Dubai World announced that it would be unable to repay its debts on time. A loan of $10 billion from Abu Dhabi at the end of the year helped Dubai avoid defaulting on its obligations. Dubai's luxury real estate market soon recovered, but some uncertainty lingered regarding the emirate's ability to pay off its debts.

The United Arab Emirates responded to the popular uprisings that swept through much of the Arab world in 2011 by preemptively tightening its control over political expression. In April 2011, five democracy activists were arrested for signing an online petition calling for an elected parliament and a constitutional monarchy. The activists were convicted and sentenced to prison for publicly insulting the country's leaders before being pardoned and released in November.

Efforts to suppress dissent continued in 2012 with the passage of new measures banning criticism of the government in public or on the Internet. Dozens of democracy activists and members of the Islamist opposition were arrested and detained without charges over the course of the year.

Foreign relations

The regime of Ruhollah Khomeini in Iran and the subsequent Iran-Iraq War (1980–88) created problems for the United Arab Emirates. The resurgence of Islamic fundamentalism posed a double threat to the federation's stability by generating unrest among the Iranian Shī'ites living in the emirates and providing inspiration to the growing numbers of young activist Sunnis, who found the existing political order unsupportive and uncommitted to upholding Islamic values.

Fighting during the Iran-Iraq War broke out within a few miles of the emirates' coast when Iran and Iraq began to attack tankers in the Persian Gulf. The intensity of such threats moved the emirates to join with Oman, Qatar, Saudi Arabia, Bahrain, and Kuwaitto form the Gulf Cooperation Council (GCC) in 1981. The council was designed to strengthen the security of its members and to promote economic cooperation. The United Arab Emirates joined Saudi Arabia and the other GCC states in condemning Iraq's invasion of Kuwait in 1990. It provided facilities for Western military forces and contributed troops for the liberation of Kuwait in early 1991. The emirates also became a member of both the United Nations and the Arab League in 1991.

The emirates, backed by fellow GCC members, objected vigorously when in 1992 Iran strengthened its control over the disputed islands of Abū Mūsa and the Tunbs (Ṭunb al-Kubrā and Ṭunb al-Ṣughrā), both seized by Iran in 1971. Iran continued to engage in development activities on the islands throughout the decade, including the establishment of an airport on Abū Mūsa and a power station on Ṭunb al-Kubrā in 1996, further straining relations between the two countries; by 2006 no conclusive resolution to these disputes had been reached. The emirates responded by moving closer to the Western powers while maintaining a confrontational stance toward Iran.

In the late 1990s the federation was one of only three countries along with Pakistan and Saudi Arabia to recognize the Taliban regime of Afghanistan. The emirates broke relations with that group in 2001, however, when the Taliban refused to extradite Islamic militant Osama bin Laden, accused of organizing the September 11, 2001, attacks on the World Trade Center in New York City and on the Pentagon outside Washington, D.C.

In early 2006 a fierce debate emerged over the move by state-owned Dubai Ports World (DP World) to take over management of a number of U.S. ports through its acquisition of the British firm that had previously run the ports. Citing security fears, the U.S. Congress threatened to block the deal, which was supported by Pres. George W. Bush. Though political confrontation was averted when DP World committed to divesting of the ports shortly thereafter, the incident provoked strong international debate. In 2007 state-backed Dubai Aerospace Enterprises was also forced to back out of its proposal to purchase a majority stake in the Auckland International Airport in New

Zealand; the deal, supported by airport board officials, was faced with overwhelming local council and public opposition.

From 2011 a major concern of the United Arab Emirates' foreign policy was to prevent the type of popular uprisings that were taking place in other Arab countries from threatening the monarchies of the Gulf region. To that end the United Arab Emirates and its allies in the GCC sent troops to Bahrain to suppress an uprising led by Bahrain's marginalized Shīʿite majority. The emirates also contributed financial assistance to the government of Bahrain and the government of Oman, which also faced protests in 2011.

In the turbulent climate that followed the popular uprisings of 2011, the United Arab Emirates began to take a more active role in regional affairs, developing its military capabilities and projecting power in new ways. In 2014 it joined the U.S.-led air campaign against the Islamic State in Iraq and the Levant (ISIL; also called ISIS) and also conducted limited air strikes in Libya. In 2015 the United Arab Emirates joined a coalition led by Saudi Arabia against Houthi rebels in Yemen. Meanwhile, Emirati commandos were deployed to the southern coast of Yemen to battle Al-Qaeda in the Arabian Peninsula. Beginning in June 2018, the United Arab Emirates took the lead in the coalition's offensive to seize Yemen's port city of Al-Ḥudaydah, a key source of revenue for the Houthis and the main point of entry for food and humanitarian aid into Yemen. The United Arab Emirates was also a key participant in a blockade of nearby Qatar beginning in 2017, a move interpreted by many as an attempt to stave off influence from political rivals in the region, especially Iran and the Muslim Brotherhood.

Emirates

Dubai

It seems like the ultra-modern city of Dubai is having a moment, Dubai is all over television and travel guides in the recent years; though if you are like many people, the long and fascinating history of this desert city may still be a mystery. Here is a brief history of Dubai, maybe it will inspire you to visit this historic and modern city.

Ancient History

Though official records of modern Dubai didn't start appearing until the 18th century, evidence of nomadic herding people date back to 3,000 C.E. From 3,000 C.E., there has been evidence of permanent farming based settlements. Archaeologists have also found evidence of large scale trading caravan outposts, leading them to believe the area was an important hub for trading during various times. During the 7th century C.E. Dubai was under the first known Muslim dynasty, the Umayyad. The Umayyad was a political and religious empire stretching from Spain to India with Arabian Peninsula firmly in the center. With increased trade routes the Dubai area began to prosper through coastal industries such as pear diving and fishing. Profits from pearl diving began to plummet in the 20th century due to a lack of demand internationally due to two world wars and the effects these had on trade routes and global economies.

Modern History

Dubai's economy relied heavily on fishing and pearl diving until the mid-20th century when Dubai struck oil in 1966. Oil changed everything for this sleepy town and eventually transformed it into the mega city it is today. Shortly after Dubai switched its currency from the rupee to the riyal (which it still uses today.) With the recent oil money, Sheikh Rashid began developing a modern a city and in 1971 the United Arab Emirates was formed with Dubai as its shiny capital. Dubai's recent history as a "planned" city has led to an incredibly clean and modern infrastructure.

Dubai Today

The Dubai of the 19th century is hardly noticeable amongst today's skyscrapers. No longer a scrabble of fishing villages, today Dubai is home to countless modern marvels including the world's tallest building (for now,) air conditioned bus stops, supercars, and massive golf courses (yes even in the middle of the desert!) While oil still accounts for most of the local's wealth (which are surprisingly only 15% of Dubai's population) tourism and real estate are becoming larger and larger pieces of Dubai's economy. Dubai is popular amongst the world's elites and is the most expensive city in the Middle East and one of the most expensive in the world. It also home to millions of immigrants from Africa and Asia who have come to desert city to work in a variety of fields.

The history of Dubai could be summed up as the story of change. From humble beginnings to one of the world's most futuristic places, Dubai has always been unique and continues to grow more and more fascinating. With daily flights via Qatar Airways there has never been a better time to explore this fascinating city. Also, Qatar Airways offer best in-flight experience, along with connecting flights to many top cities across the Globe.

Dubai Culture

Culture in Dubai is rooted in Islamic traditions that form UAE National's lifestyles. It is highly important that when tourists visit Dubai they must respect and behave suitably, as the minority group of Emiratis are very protective over their culture and traditions.

Dubai is famously known as the entertainment capital of the Middle East which attracts many party lovers from all over the world, especially those who are wealthy enough to splash out on the most expensive places in the city. With Dubai promoting such an image, it still forbids the nationals that practice Islam to indulge in any of the entertaining services offered. In that respect these services are often located in the more touristy areas rather than in residential parts.

Alcohol is not forbidden in Dubai, as long as it is confined within an area like a hotel, bar or nightclub. Residents are free to drink in their own homes as long as they have an alcohol licence issued by the municipality. It is illegal to drink in the street or in public places. Pork is also available for the consumption of visitors and expatriates.

It is advised that visitors and expatriates do not flaunt their Western culture habits in the streets, where they can be viewed by nationals who may find it offensive. There have been various complaints in the past by nationals who have expressed their views through the media about their home-land being taken over by the Western world.

Having said this, it does not mean the locals are against foreigners visiting Dubai, it is just common courtesy to respect your hosts. Emiratis are traditionally known for their warm hospitality and they are very generous when offering refreshments to guests.

Emiratis tend to dress in their traditional clothes influenced by their Islamic belief. Most men prefer the traditional dishdasha or khandura (a long white shirt-dress), with ghutra (a white headdress) and agal (a rope worn to keep the ghutra in place). The Emirati women tend to wear an abaya (a long black cloak), which is worn over conservative clothes, with a sheyla or hijab (a scarf used to wrap around the face and head).

Expatriates and visitors are advised to dress appropriately; trousers or a dress should be worn to cover below the knee, when circulating the city, especially at historical sites. However, they can wear what they wish when they are in a hotel, bar or club and swim wear is tolerated by the pool or at the beach.

Normally tourist photography is acceptable and expected with all the beauty Dubai has to offer. Photographs of government buildings, military installations, ports and airports should not be taken. Like anywhere, it is polite to ask permission before photographing people, especially an Emirati woman.

Religion

The most religious time of the year in Dubai, is the fast of Ramadan, which lasts approximately for one month. This is when Muslims fast during day-light hours to fulfil the fourth pillar of Islam. Tourists must be aware that during this period, eating, drinking and smoking is not permitted in public during the day, although some restaurants blackout their windows to allow people to consume in private. Also bars will not serve alcohol before 7pm and clubs are shut as no loud music is allowed. The UAE is tolerant and welcoming to foreigners who do not practice the religion of Islam. For example, the huge Arab population in Dubai includes many from Lebanon that can be of Christian faith and they are freely allowed to follow their own religion as long as they do not publicly distribute their literature. This also applies to any other non-Muslim expatriates.

Once in the city of Dubai you are surrounded by many mosques and the call of prayer will be heard frequently. The city also accommodates other religious places of worship, such as churches and Temples

The government follows a policy of tolerance towards non-Muslims and Polytheist and in practice, interferes very little with their religious activities.

Dubai is the only emirate that has Hindu temples and a Sikh gurudwara. The Meena Bazaar area of the city has both a Shiva and Krishna temple. Both are believed to be sanctioned by the late ruler of Dubai, Sheikh Rashid Bin Saeed Al Maktoum. There is an electric crematorium run by a group of Indian expatriates. Furthermore, in early 2001, ground was broken for the construction of several additional churches on a parcel of land in Jebel Ali donated by the government of Dubai for four Protestant congregations and a Catholic congregation. Construction on the first Greek Orthodox Church in Dubai (to be called St. Mary's) is due for completion in 2008/9, with the help of General Sheikh Mohammad Bin Rashid Al Maktoum, Dubai Crown Prince and UAE Defence Minister, who donated a plot of land in Jebel Ali.

Language

The official language of the country is Arabic, however most people in and out of the workplace communicate in English. There are so many different nationalities in Dubai and therefore English finds common ground with most people. The majority of road, shop signs, and restaurant menus etc. are in both English and Arabic.

Sights in Dubai

Burj Al Arab

The Burj's graceful silhouette – meant to evoke the sail of a dhow (a traditional wooden cargo vessel) – is to Dubai what the Eiffel Tower is to Paris. Completed in 1999, this iconic landmark sits on an artificial island and comes with its own helipad and a fleet of chauffeur-driven Rolls Royce limousines. Beyond the striking lobby, with its gold-leaf opulence and attention-grabbing fountain, lie 202 suites with more trimmings than a Christmas turkey.

It's worth visiting if only to gawk at an interior that's every bit as garish as the exterior is gorgeous. The mood is set in the 180m-high lobby, which is decorated in a red, blue and green colour scheme and accented with pillars draped in gold leaf. The lobby atrium is tall enough to fit the Statue of Liberty within it.

If you're not staying in the hotel, you need a restaurant reservation to get past lobby security. Don't expect any bargains: there's a minimum spend of Dhs370 for cocktails in the Skyview Bar, while afternoon tea will set you back Dhs590. Check the website for details and to make a (compulsory) reservation.

Note that some refurbishments will be taking place in 2019, so there may be temporary closures.

Al Bastakiya

There are a handful of Dubai monuments that showcase the traditional Dubai and Bastakia Quarter or Al Bastakiya is one of them. Comfortably standing between the Dubai Creek and Bur Dubai, the neighborhood is a mini maze of art galleries, museums, cafes, and buildings. Sauntering through the sand-colored, narrow lanes of the heritage area, you will notice wind towers on most buildings. These towers acted as natural air-conditioners back in the day and still keep the place relatively cooler. One can't help but appreciate how beautifully the site has been restored, especially after the year 1970, when it was in shambles, and some people wanted to see it demolished. This is a cherished part of Dubai's history and a highly recommended tourist attraction, enough to evoke the explorer in you.

Ferrari World

An adventurous escapade awaits as you drive an hour from Dubai and reach the Yas Island located in Abu Dhabi, a part of the United Arab Emirates. One of the most popular weekend getaways in the area, Yas

Island is picking up as a world-known attraction for leisure and entertainment with a jiff of adventure. However, the prime attraction of the island is Ferrari world- an entertainment park in the Yas Marina Circuit. Touted as the largest indoor theme park in the world, Ferrari World is the first and only Ferrari-branded park in the world that offers thrilling rides, exciting attractions, themed stores and restaurants, all inspired by the valuable Ferrari brand and its Italian heritage. The park possesses more than 20 unique rides and attractions for visitors of all ages, but the most loved and exciting of the lot is Formula Rossa, world's fastest roller coaster.

Saeed Al Maktoum House

The perfect spot to time travel, Saeed Al Maktoum House is believed to be one of the oldest buildings in Dubai and the ancestral home of the current ruler of the emirate, His Highness Sheikh Mohammed bin Rashid Al Maktoum. An appropriate example of the traditional architecture of Dubai, climb to the top tower of the structure to experience the magnificence of the Dubai skyline. It is now a museum containing documents, photographs, stamps, and coins sharing the story of Dubai's history and its transformation into a modern and a superlatively developed nation. History lovers, you're in for a treat! One could spend hours appreciating Dubai's local heritage.

Al Quoz

A rather interesting locality in Dubai, Al Quoz is an industrial neighborhood that has beautifully developed the contemporary art scene in Dubai. This is also the location of the first private museum in Dubai, the Salsali Private Museum. Some of the noteworthy galleries include Van den Eynde Gallery, Carbon 12 Dubai, et al. You will also find a place called Satellite at Al Quoz, which is an alternative art space that promotes art by inviting regional and international artists to the gallery to produce and develop original artwork. Functioning on similar lines is The Fridge, a performing arts center in the neighboring area that promotes and gives a platform to regional musicians and performance artists. Spend some 'arty' time at the destination learning all about Dubai's art and music scene.

Jumeirah Beach

A jewel in Dubai's crown, the Jumeirah Beach is a prime tourist attraction and one of the most beautiful places in the city. The spectacular white sand beach also has a beach park. You can walk on the grass and get a perfect view of the ever-changing Dubai skyline. There are enough restaurants and cafes on the beach that offer lip smacking food. If you're traveling with kids, put your worries to rest. There is a children's play area to keep your toddlers entertained. Other than that, very close to the beach is Jumeirah Mosque, one of the few mosques in the UAE that is open to non-Muslims. It allows you to get insights into Islamic culture and traditions. It can be visited on all days except Friday. Another place that deserves a visit while at the Jumeirah is The Walk at the Beach Residence. Buzzing with activity on a general day, this is city's first outdoor promenade with hundreds of cafes and restaurants, supermarkets, boutiques. After spending an eventful day at this place, relax at the close by Jumeirah Beach Residence Open Beach.

Dubai Heritage Village

Also known as the Hatta Village, the Dubai Heritage Village is a collection of mud and stone houses, palm trees and gives you a glimpse into of the Emirati folk culture in the Middle East. The old-world charm exuded by the place keeps a visitor fascinated, and this place also gives you insights into the different aspects of leading a local life ranging from coastal to mountains. A rather interesting feature of the village is that it exhibits traditional professions of the emirate including blacksmithing, jewelry making, cotton trading, et al. A person can also buy artifacts and other items like tools, equipment, and traditional sweets. A 200-year-old mosque, weapon rooms and resting cafes that have been here since the 16th century- this place will make you time travel and enjoy the aura of the 16th century in the 21st century.

The Dubai Fountain

Picture this- Casually strolling around the Dubai Mall, ready to call it a day when suddenly the fountains around you break into a dance performance! No, these aren't the words of a delusional mind, but the sight every day at the Dubai Mall- thanks to The Dubai Fountain. Known to be the world's largest choreographed water system, the water of the fountain is illuminated by more than 6,600 lights in 25 different colors. The water from the sprinklers is shot up as high as 500 feet and lasts up to 5 minutes with a wide genre of music from classical to contemporary Arabic to world music playing in the background. The fountains have been set on the 30-acre, manmade Burj Khalifa Lake and such is the grandeur of dance, it is visible not only from every corner of the promenade, but also from the neighbouring structures.

Grand Mosque

The current structure may only be as old as 1998, but the Grand Mosque- the tallest minaret in Dubai- was originally built in 1900, demolished soon after and then rebuilt in 1960. After much reconstruction and restoration, the final structure was erected in 1998 and has been the same ever since. The mosque is not open to non-Muslims, but they can enter the minaret where photography is permitted. This mosque is often touted to as the center of cultural and religious belief of Dubai.

Dubai Zoo

Dubai Zoo is often referred to as the oldest of its kind not only in the United Arab Emirates but all of Arabian Peninsula. First opened in 1967, it later came under the management of Dubai Municipality in 1971 and has constantly been renovated and reinvented ever since. It was the first zoo in the emirate to breed the rare Chimpanzee and the Arabian Wild Cat. Other than that, the zoo houses more than 250 species of animals including Asiatic Lions, Jaguars, Giraffes, Barbary Sheeps, et al. Some of the rarest of rare animals like Bengal Tiger, subspecies of grey wolf, Socotra shag can also be spotted in the zoo. A one-stop destination for children and adults, Dubai Zoo, is the choicest tourist spot for everyone.

Dubai Butterfly Garden

The most recent entry to Dubai's tourist attractions is the Dubai Butterfly Garden. Located alongside the Dubai Miracle Garden, this place is home to thousands of beautiful and colourful butterflies. As soon as a tourist enters the park, they can explore the butterfly and insect museum. As they move along, they see nine domes made in different colours, home to 24 different types of butterflies from various countries. Other than that, there is a pond where you can find fishes in vibrant hues. A visitor can learn a lot about the anatomy of butterflies and gain insights about their life cycle and metamorphosis.

Grab a bite at the coffee shop at the park and shop for some souvenirs for your folks and friends at the end of your visit.

Legoland Dubai

A interactive and fun theme park, Legoland is a must-visit place of attraction for families with children aged between 2 and 12. With over 40 Lego themed ride, shows, experiences and attractions, the park is said to keep kids interested like no place else. Build a Lego car and test it against an opponent or build a building and prove it mettle in an earthquake at Build and Test and let your kids aged between 6 and 13 have a real life driving experience at the Lego Driving School. Toddlers enjoy the Duplo Valley, especially the Duplo Express a small train ride. While you are here sign up for a fun tutorial to build and program a cutting edge robot that obeys your every command, recover stolen treasures by blasting targets with laser guns at the Lost Kingdom Adventure, and dodge surprise water blasts and power ski through waves at Wave Racer. Take a fun Factory Tour and learn how Lego Bricks are produced and spend quality time with your kids in the indoor building and education area called the Lego Master Builder Academy - the place has a lot more to offer than what meets the eye!

Aquaventure Waterpark

Laid out across two main towers- Poseidon and Neptune, Aquaventure Waterpark has a collection of adrenalin-pumping rides. While Tower of Neptune is all about overcoming the unseen tunnel adventures and braving the Shark Lagoon, the Tower of Poseidon is the battle with the King of the Sea. This place is also home to World's largest water slide, the Aquaconda. A tourist needs to remember that they need to follow the swim attire policy of the park in order to be allowed to use all the rides of the park. A perfect setup for an adventure, Aquaventure Waterpark can be your favorite day in Dubai, depending on your love for an exciting escapade.

IMG Worlds of Adventures

Dubai's first indoor mega themed entertainment destination, IMG Worlds of Adventure is an adventure and fun zone for visitors of all ages. It has four epic adventure zones in one location with themes like Cartoon Network, MARVEL, Lost Valley, and IMG Boulevard. The zones feature an array of adrenaline-pumping roller coasters, thrill rides, spine-tingling attractions, exclusive retail stores, state-of-the-art cinemas, and memorable dining experiences. Earn yourself a place among The Avengers as you team up with Iron Man, Hulk, Captain America and Hawkeye to fight the battle of the Age of Ultron and be rescued from the clutches of Loki, the God of Mischief as Thor and the mighty avengers battle their way to see you safe. Enter the Lost Valley and take a ride on The Velociraptor, not for the faint hearted, this thrill ride launches from prehistoric jungles to the deserts of Dubai itself. Stop by the Adventure Fortress and learn the skills needed to protect the village from dinosaurs, there are tunnels to cross, and bridges to conquer, nets to tackle and challenges to take - it's an experience like no other. Kids have an amazing time in the Cartoon Network themed park as they ride on Mojo Jojo's Robot Rampage, and the IMG Boulevard offers the experience of a Haunted Restaurant.

Dubai Frame

Believed to be the world's largest picture frame, the Dubai Frame is a 150 meter tall and 93 meter wide hollow, gold-plated, observation tower. Situated in the Zabeel Park, this tower gives you a quick glimpse into the city of Dubai, covering both the old and the new city. When you look south, you see the modern Dubai with high rise buildings and enormous skyscrapers including the Burj Khalifa, the world's tallest building and the Emirates Towers. The north view on the other side offers a view of some of the historic neighbourhoods of the city like Deira, Umm Harare, and Karama among others. The glass-bottomed skydeck a 360 degree view of the city and its magnificence and you should definitely not miss it on your trip to Dubai. There is also a museum on its lower floors and you can see the past, present, and future of Dubai here. Right from what it used to be, a sleepy fishing village to the global destination that it is today, to what it aspires to be by the year 2050.

Motiongate

Enjoy a day filled with Hollywood entertainment from three of the largest and most successful motion pictures studios - DreamWorks Animation, Columbia Pictures, and Lionsgate as you enter a world of wonder and impressive storytelling. Join the Ghostbusters in a paranormal battle to save the New York City and embark on a high-speed chase Green Hornet style. Join the Furious Five on an epic martial arts escapade, and play the hero and save the day at attractions like the Kung Fu Panda, Shrek, and How to Train Your Dragon. Visit the Smurfs Village and enjoy your time in the fairytale mushroom-top houses and have an exciting time with your family at its charming theatre show. Take the Capitol Bullet Train inspired by the movie The Hunger Games, and have a blast off at Zombie Land. Families have a wonderful time at The Fountain of Dreams and Kung Fu Panda's Unstoppable Awesomeness Ride, and young adults can be thrilled on epic rides like the Madagascar Mad Pursuit and the Dragon Gliders. For tourists looking to enjoy a splash, The Cloudy With A Chance of Meatballs - River Expedition will provide for fun unlimited. Motiongate also offers live entertainment and outdoor shows that ensure that there is never a dull moment here.

Dubai Creek

In the heart of Dubai lies Dubai Creek- a saltwater creek that separates Bur Dhabi and Deira. To witness the outrageous magnificence of this city, take a cruise in the traditional Arab dhows that can be easily spotted floating across waters. It's a pocket-friendly ride that allows a beautiful view of the city in a few minutes. Passing through the shimmering waters of the creek, you can see the historical construction of the emirate on one end and the modernity of the city on another. Adding to the clamor of the activity on the dhow are the lively souks that can be spotted from a distance that gives you insights into the marine-time trade of Dubai, first hand.

Wild Wadi Water Park

Having taken inspiration from a popular character in Arabic folklore, Juha, The Wild Wadi Water Park is an entertainment, water theme park in Dubai. It is a highly enjoyable experience for families that frequent this tourist attraction. Known for some rather unique rides, your visit to the theme park will include a rendezvous with a hot wave pool, and a cool one too, artificial surfing machines, waterfalls, et al. Other known water slides that shouldn't be missed are the Master Blaster, Tantrum Alley, and Burj Surj. The 30 rides at the park will give you the quite an adrenaline rush and could also be one of your most adventurous experiences. Complete the visit by grabbing a scrumptious bite at one of the three restaurants available on the premises.

Pro Tip: The special price for UAE residents may vary from time to time. Please visit the official website to check for rates

Sharjah

Another city in the UAE, Sharjah is Dubai's Emirati brother and an entire entity in itself. You may have to extend your trip for a day or two to make the most of this place, considering it is the third largest city in the UAE after Dubai and Abu Dhabi. A tourist can get insights into the heritage of UAE with a lot of monuments and old structures that have been restored. Art and history lovers are also in for a treat, thanks to the extensive collection of museums and galleries including Sharjah Art Museum, Sharjah Calligraphy Museum, and Sharjah Archeology Museum among others. Shop, eat, make merry and indulge in some cool adventure activities while visiting this exciting place.

Wadi Bih

If you are remotely adventurous and wish to trek or camp in a rugged terrain, Wadi Bih is your go-to place. Known in Dubai for the relay race that's conducted every year, the place has an exotic view of dangerous, yet achievable trails that are sure to set your pulse racing. Once you have trumped a certain distance, fix your tent at any location and revel in nature's glory with the breathtaking view of this terrain. Wadi Bih is an offbeat destination in the outskirts of Dubai and is a relatively lesser crowded tourist destination.

Creek Park

What may sound like just another garden in Dubai, Creek Park goes a step ahead in elevating the travel experience of a tourist. The large park houses within its premises, verdant stretches, theme parks and flower beds that make you feel close to the true beauty of nature. There is also a barbecue area at the park where more often that not, you will find a gathering of people, making the most of great weather and roasting themselves a delicious meal. Rent a bike to drive around the park and get the most out of its beautiful surroundings. After having explored the ground, it's time to take the flight! Head to the 2.3-kilometer long cable car stretch that you can cover in a matter of 30 minutes. Suspended in air for that long, you can gaze far and wide and treat your eyes with the magnificent Dubai skyline.

Burj Khalifa

Rightfully the most popular tourist attraction in Dubai, the Burj Khalifa has to its name, the title of being the tallest building in the world. It looks mammoth and almost unreachable when you gaze at it from below. So once you reach the observation deck on the 124th floor, it makes you feel nothing less than surreal. Allowing a panoramic view of the Dubai skyline, you can also watch a multi-media presentation on Dubai and the building as a part of your visit to the deck. Judging from the experience of most tourists, it is best if you visit this monument in the dark of the night. The city is adorned with lights glimmering with color, which is a sight that will be etched in your memory forever.

Pro Tip: Prime hours of visit are subject to changeThe place is accessible for disabled guests

Children's City

The Children's City is the first educational park in the UAE for children between the age of two to fifteen years. Made for the holistic entertainment, the city goes a step ahead and allows the child to explore, discover, and learn about the world in which we live. Situated in Dubai Creek, it is designed to promote children interaction with family and school groups. Of the several exhibits, the popular ones include a simulator where you can fly on a magic carpet or ride a camel, programs like space exploration, the human body, computer & communication and planetarium workshops. The city is well bifurcated to suit the needs of children and adults alike. While the elders can try their hand at sending out messages using giant computers, the toddlers can spend time in the kids zone. A great place to spend a day, Children's City should be on your list of must-visit places when vacationing at Dubai.

The Lost Chambers Aquarium

The Lost City of Atlantis. 10 Chambers. Unparalleled Marine Life. Get ready for an underwater adventure, an experience of a lifetime, as you visit The Lost Chambers Aquarium in the grand, Atlantis The Palm hotel in Dubai. Based on the theme of lost city of Atlantis, walking through the 10 underground water chambers, you will witness shipwrecks and ruins of a lost civilization used by unique marine animals to play peekaboo with their visitors. Fish including sharks, piranha, stingrays and lobsters, et al. are all a part of this world that has been beautifully erected at the Atlantis. Become a part of one of their exclusive tour to get the first-hand experience at picking up a starfish or caressing a sea cucumber. You can also join the Behind The Scene Tour to unravel the secrets of the deep. If you still aren't satisfied, reach out to the animal experts and help them in feeding some of the marine animals yourself.

Dubai Garden Glow

One of Dubai's favourite family destinations, the Dubai Garden Glow is a magical theme park with unique concepts that entertain visitors of all ages. With attractions including a Dinosaur Park, an Ice Park, a Glow Park, the Happy Forest, and the Happiness Street, the park has creative installations, live musical shows, and performances by some of the best talents in UAE. Experience a kaleidoscopic world with laser effects, light shows, and a stunning ambiance at the Colourful World, and enjoy a user engagement experience with cutting-edge technology that captures visitors in the enchanting 'sea world' and its charm. Stop by the Magical Nights Glow Park and be amazed by the colourful lanterns, illuminated animal sculptures inspired by wildlife and intricately crafted sculptures with nature landscape representations. Contrasting to the desert atmosphere outside, the Ice Park offers an outrageous ambience with skillfully crafted ice sculptures of Mini Dubai, Ice Age, and a Children's Play area. When in Dubai, this place is a sure must- visit for every tourist that is smitten by colours and art.

Dubai Miracle Garden

It must be some piece of art if a place is called the world's biggest natural flower garden. This is the case with Dubai Miracle Garden, which was inaugurated on 14th February 2013 as a tribute to love. A new addition to Dubai's tourist's spots, the Miracle Garden, true to its name, is nothing short of a miracle. It has over 45 million flowers put together in different shapes and sizes like igloos, pyramids, hearts, et al. The floral display gets a new look every season and with the changing months, the flowers on display also change color and shape. This way, it is ensured that a visitor travelling to the place more than once, gets to see something new with every visit. Don't shake your head in disbelief; visit the site to know that it actually happens.

Dubai Festival City

A combination of residential, business and entertainment complexes, the Dubai Festival City is often referred to as a city within the city. The place has a lot to offer to a tourist- fine-dining restaurants, casual bistros, comfortable cafes and world-class retailers. A visitor can also catch an event or two at the Novo Festival Cinemas complex or shop to their hearts content at the multiple showrooms across the city. It boasts of some of the best and world-known brands available here. Another thing that keeps getting a traveler back to it is that it is also touted as the place in the emirate with the most photographed sunset vistas.

Abu Dhabi

Abu Dhabi's people today enjoy living in modern, technologically advanced surroundings, a huge historic leap from living in simple mud-brick huts like some of its previous settlers.

The emirate is rich in archeological finds. There has been evidence that the very first settlements were from the 3rd millennium BC in some regions of Abu Dhabi. Its early history resembles that of the nomadic period with typical herding and fishing lifestyles.

Settlements can be traced back as far as over 5000 years ago, and have been found around parts of Abu Dhabi, such as Jebel Hafeet near Al Ain and on the island of Umm al Nar.

Abu Dhabi's most significant settlement was those of the Bani Yas Bedoiun tribe which were located by the coast around the 16th Century. Afterwards, the discovery of fresh water led the tribe to relocate to the island which was more fertile with large quantities of wildlife. Soon after, the ruling Al Nahyan family decided to flee to the island also.

Under the rule of Sheikh Zayed bin Khalifa, Abu Dhabi thoroughly developed through the trading of pearls, and in 1892 came the very first exclusive treaty linking Abu Dhabi with Great Britain. The emirates location was seen as a great strategic convenience connecting it with India and the east, and it was established as the Trucial coast.

Whilst Abu Dhabi's wealth was looking on the upside, it was badly hit by the intervention of Japan's pearl industry and also by the 1930's global recession. Furthermore, Sheik Zayed bin Khalifa passed away which added more uncertainty to Abu Dhabi's prosperity.

However, this was not the end of Abu Dhabi's fortunes. In 1939 Sheikh Shakhbut bin Sultan Al Nahyan granted petroleum concession to the Trucial Coast Development Oil Company, (renamed the Abu Dhabi Petroleum Company, ADPC, in 1962) in a bid to search for large oil reserves. In 1958, huge offshore oil reserves were discovered and a year later onshore reserves were also found. It was not until 1962 that the oil exports began, leading Abu Dhabi on to the road of unbelievable wealth.

In 1966 Sheik Zayed bin Sultan Al Nahyan became the new ruler of Abu Dhabi and two years later he formed the federation of the United Arab Emirates, which was in response to the British threatening to withdraw from the region by the end of 1971. The ruler of Abu Dhabi realised that his connection with Britain was vital in order to maintain a strong position in the oil industry. Sheikh Zayed bin Sultan Al Nahayan was elected as the first president and with the assistance of the British started to carry out his vision of developing the country with the advantage of increased oil revenues.

Sheikh Zayed was known as the 'Father of the Nation' due to his great developments of the city of Abu Dhabi. Unfortunately he passed away in 2004 and his son Sheik Khalifa bin Zayed Al Nahyan was elected as president and made sure he would continue his father's legacy.

Sheik Khalifa has invested oil reserves sensibly in order to boost tourism figures. With the outstanding determination of the Al Nahyan family reign, anything is possible.

Key fascinating and impressive developments have been implemented, such as the Saadiyat Island and Al Grum Resort in order to attract visitors from all over the globe.

Abu Dhabi, the capital of the UAE, has come a long way; rapidly re-constructing itself into a flawless city, with extraordinary sky scrapers, shopping malls, top quality hotels and picturesque gardens. It is certainly very different from what it was 50 years ago, but its history still remains a prominent factor in its path to success.

Culture

Abu Dhabi has been converted into a tourist attraction, an up-to-date city with its sophisticated high rise buildings, extensive entertainment facilities and beautiful large gardens and parks. However, beneath this modern portrayal lies a rich cultural background.

The emirate's culture is strongly embedded within the Islamic traditions of Arabia, with many mosques scattered around the city amongst the modern architecture. Abu Dhabi consists of many nationalities and cultures, which are all welcomed as long as they do not jeopardise the Islamic religion. Although the city has changed dramatically in the last 40 years by foreign influences, the people of Abu Dhabi still uphold old traditions and continue to promote their cultures to those unaware of their prosperous heritage.

Abu Dhabi is known as the cultural heart of the UAE, enthusiastically marketing cultural and sporting events that represent its past. Sports include, camel racing and dhow sailing, and cultural events include Arabic poetry, dances and music.

Many locals dress traditionally, men in their full length shirt-dress (dishdasha) with a white or red checked head dress (gutra), whilst women wear a black abaya – a long black robe and a headscarf (sheyla).

The official national language of Abu Dhabi is Arabic, although, English, Hindi and Urdu are also widely spoken in and around the city.

Sights

Yas Island

One of the top luxury hotel destinations in Abu Dhabi is Yas Island. The island has huge stretches of the sandy beach making it ideal for spending the day sunbathing. It is an emerging destination that is a mere 30-minute drive from the capital city of Abu Dhabi. The island is also a home to Marina Circuit where the F1 racing of Abu Dhabi takes place. The development project of the island was started out in the year 2006 with the aim of metamorphosing the island into a multi-purpose leisure spot that gave the tourists the finest choice in shopping, eating or simply entertainment. It has been over 10 years since, and the island is entertaining both the locals and the tourists who come venturing the place.

St Andrew's Church

There are a few churches in Abu Dhabi and St. Andrews Church is one of them. A number of important Christian rituals take place at this church that makes it a valuable landmark in the city. You can visit St. Andrews Church so as to admire the lovely architecture and ambience that will fill your soul with a different energy. St. Andrews Church is also visited by foreign tourists due to its impressive interior. Marriages are held at this church and frequently accessed for several prayer meetings. You can attend the evening mass that is very vibrant. One can reach St. Andrews Church easily via public transport. Make sure you do not make noise inside the church.

Pro Tip: Do attend the evening mass

Al Wathba Wetland Reserve

Al Wathba Wetland Reserve is a wonderful place that is managed in an area away from the city. There are a number of birds such as flamingos which can be spotted in this area. The scenic beauty of Al Wathba Wetland Reserve is very mesmerizing. You can travel to this place to spend a picnic session with friends and family. This biological park is not accessed by the common people. You need to plan a proper trip to visit this place. Al Wathba Wetland Reserve is not open on all days which make the access to this destination more difficult. Make sure you carry excess drinking water on your journey

Emirates National Auto Museum

One of the most prominent sightseeing attraction in the Abu Dhabi is the Emirates National Auto Museum. It is a privately owned museum the building of which is structured in the form of the modern day pyramid and is situated 45 kilometers towards the south of the Abu Dhabi city in the United Arab Emirates. The museum stocks some 200 different exhibition items that are on display for the visitors to see. Emirates National Auto Museum's incredible collection consists of a huge variety of sports cars, military vehicles, towable caravans, and a lot more. Besides this, there is a massive compilation of the off-road vehicles including the Sheikh's Mercedes rainbow collection and classic American cars among others.

Historical Context: The collection of the Emirates National Auto Museum was featured in the BBC television programme Top Gear.

Pro Tip: Though the museum is open all days of the week but the opening hours are subject to change. So do confirm the opening time before undertaking the trip.

Sheikh Zayed Grand Mosque

Sheikh Zayed Grand Mosque is Abu Dhabi's landmark building. This splendid and absolute mammoth mosque fuses the design elements of Ottoman, Mameluk, and Fatamid in order to create a modern mosque that well celebrates the architecture of Islam. Artisans made use of mosaic tiling, glass work, and some intricate carvings so as to give a beautiful effect on both exteriors as well as the interior of the mosque. The mosque was opened to the public in the year 2007- nearly 2 decades post its construction. It has a massive capacity and can accommodate some 40,000 worshippers thereby making it the biggest mosque in the whole of the United Arab Emirates. For first timers, there are guided tours available to explore the mosque.

Historical Context: The mosque is dedicated to Late Shelkh Zayed Bin Sultan al-Nahyan.

Pro Tip: Dress appropriately when visiting the mosque.

Masdar City

Masdar City is a must-visit section of Abu Dhabi due to its environment-friendly activities. The main aim is to become a 0 Carbon region. There are numerous efforts made to utilize renewable energy to run Masdar City. There are solar panels installed in different locations along with self-driving cars that are very amusing. Masdar City is a protected section of Abu Dhabi that is basically an experiment for a future world that is quite systematic in terms of sustainable development. You can tour this area and check out restaurants as well that offer organic food. This is indeed an interesting destination that shouldn't be missed when you are in the city of Abu Dhabi.

Pro Tip: Do try the organic food

About Yas Waterworld

In the heat dome of the Middle East, the one thing that does offer respite and a chilling thrill from the scorching heat is the Yas Waterworld. Indulge in some exciting rides, slides, and attractions at this beautiful water park. Located next to the Ferrari World, this water park is spread over an area of 15 hectares of land. At this water park, you can enjoy some of the wettest and the steepest rides in the United Arab Emirates. There is a total of 45 different rides to help you enjoy the awesome fun at this water park. The Yas Waterworld was started in the year 2013, and even in this short span of 3 years, the theme park has become one of the most popular tourist attraction in the Middle East.

Pro Tip: All the single ladies must watch out for the ladies night on Thursday from 6:00 PM to 11:00 PM

About Abu Dhabi Falcon Hospital

One of the most obscure attractions in Abu Dhabi is its Falcon Hospital. This animal care unit is focused towards the health of the Falcons. Falcons have been an important part of the Emirati society and Falconry has long been practiced in the UAE. As of today, Falconry has rather become a sport and no longer a necessity as hunting is strictly prohibited in the city. However, Falcons are still revered, and the healthcare of the Falcons is the main object of the hospital. It was opened in the year 1999, and ever since then, it has been caring for over 8500 falcons every year. For anyone who is interested in learning about the Falconry can attend the two hours or the three hours guided tour of the hospital.

Historical Context: Domesticated falcons are provided their own passports in UAE.

Eastern Mangrove Lagoon National Park

You can hire a private boat in order to explore the beauty of Eastern Mangrove Lagoon National Park. You can paddle through the water to spend a lovely time in this calm environment. A number of families visit Eastern Mangrove Lagoon National Park for planning a picnic. The surrounding area of Eastern Mangrove Lagoon National Park is full of trees and wildlife. Make sure you hire a guide when visiting this place. There are kayaking tours which are also organized in this area for adventure enthusiasts. It is a peaceful destination that will surely please your senses. Carry food and water during your trip to Eastern Mangrove Lagoon National Park.

Pro Tip: Good place to watch the sunset

Corniche Beach

The Corniche Beach attracts a wide range of tourists from across the world who come here to have fun and enjoy some precious time. It is divided into three distinct areas for singles, families and the general public. Under these three sections, only the entry for the public is free while the others are paid. On the beach, you can find ample space for parking and the changing rooms. Further, facilities such as umbrellas are available that are chargeable at AED 25. On the beach, you can find a variety of delightful restaurants where you can taste some lipsmacking Arabian dishes. Other prominent attractions like the

Presidential Palace and the Marina Mall are also located near to the beach.

Historical Context: Before the 1970s, the current area of the beach was the place where the dows and the ships used to transfer people or cargo.
Pro Tip: To best explore the beach you must hire a bicycle from one of the rental shops here.

Observation Deck at 300

Situated on the 74th floor of the Tower 2 at the 300 Etihad Towers Complex is the Observation Deck, commonly known as the Observation Deck 300 that offers the beautiful views of the surrounding islands as well as the cityscape of Abu Dhabi. It is the capital's highest vantage point where 300 actually stands for the meters in the air. From such a height, one can explore the sights of the city while enjoying the light snacks, refreshments, and the delicious High Tea. If you are staying in the hotel, you do not have to pay anything to venture the Observation Deck, however, for all the nonguests of the hotel, there is an entry fee, the ticket price of which can be redeemed for the F & B vouchers at the restaurants of the deck.

Pro Tip: Dress code of the place is Business-Casual.

Yas Marina Circuit

If you wish to have a lovely driving experience in Abu Dhabi, then do visit Yas Marina Circuit. The race track is well maintained and offers a smooth run. There is a control room in the vicinity along with pit lanes. Yas Marina Circuit is a proper Grand Prix track, which is accessed by professional racers as well as local people who wish to try their hand at speed racing. Formula 1 race is held at Yas Marina Circuit that adds to its popularity and is buzzing with tourist activity during the event. You can visit this place on a guided tour that will help you access behind -the-scene areas. You can explore the cars and other aspects of this track that will surely amuse you.

Pro Tip: The behind the scene tour is amazing

Heritage Village

The Heritage Village offers the visitors and tourists a microcosm of the tradition, lifestyle and the culture of the United Arab Emirates before the oil boom. It is located near the Marina Mall at the Abu Dhabi Marina. With its close proximity to the Lulu Island, the village offers views of the Abu Dhabi Corniche. It is a great family attraction with a lot of fun things to do especially with the kids. You can find the set up of the Bedouin Ted with the camp fires brewing up the much popular Arabian Tea. The children will definitely love the Arabian horses, camels as well as the goats that are put on display here. Several artisans that exhibit the local arts can also be found here.

Pro Tip: Shop for some traditional handicrafts here.

Zayed Heritage Center

To take a fascinating sneak peek into the life of the Father of the Nation of the Abu Dhabi emirate, Sheikh Zayed, you must definitely visit the Zayed Heritage Center in the Al Bateen District. Housed in the Emirati Heritage Village, the museum or the research center is replete with camels. It offers an incredible homage to Sheikh Zayed, the man who shaped the nation. Inside the museum is the photo gallery of the Sheikh Zayed as well as the several visiting international and regional dignitaries and royalty lines adorning the beautiful walls of the museum. The museum is also decorated with the personal memorabilia like the favorite hunting rifles. Towards the center of the museum is the President's cherished vehicles that were often driven by him throughout the city without the bodyguard.

Delma Park

A relatively recent, yet popular tourist spot in Abu Dhabi is Delma Park. This place is for both adult and kids so as to spend a good time surrounded by plants and trees. People visit Delma Park in the morning and evening time to jog and spend some time in a green environment. There are a number of swings, slides and even climbing areas that are perfect for kids. There is no entry fee to this park that makes it easily accessible. The setup of Delma Park is quite comfortable that makes it more accessible and welcoming. There are food stalls close to the park area that offer interesting snack items. Make sure you do not litter the premises as it is strictly prohibited.

Pro Tip: Good place for picnics

Sheikh Zayed Cricket Stadium

Sheikh Zayed Cricket Stadium will entice cricket lovers due to its marvelous setup, and impress a non-lover with its grandeur. This place has hosted a number of cricket matches that makes it so famous. The pitch at Sheikh Zayed Cricket Stadium is quite hard which is good for bowling. Pakistan cricket team has played a number of international matches at Sheikh Zayed Cricket Stadium. This stadium is counted as one of the most celebrated destinations for modern cricket in UAE. You will love the ambiance along with arrangements at Sheikh Zayed Cricket Stadium. The seating space is very huge that can accommodate a large crowd on match days. You can reach Sheikh Zayed Cricket Stadium easily via public transport.

Pro Tip: The stadium tour is very interesting

Kidoos Entertainment

Kidoos Entertainment is an entertainment park that offers a number of rides to the kids. Apart from the rides, there are numerous adventure tasks such as climbing and sliding that are loved by the little ones. You will love the place as it is managed in a wonderful manner to please the kids. This is a good destination in Abu Dhabi that can be visited on weekends so as to surprise your little ones. Make sure your child is ready to take active participation in all the tasks offered at this place. The main focus of Kidoos Entertainment is to charge up the child's learning capabilities. The price is very decent which won't hurt your pocket.

Pro Tip: Carry a city map to reach this place

Etihad Modern Art Gallery

Etihad Modern Art Gallery is a superb place to experience modern art at its best. You can check out the work managed by renowned as well as budding artists in UAE. Etihad Modern Art Gallery is also rich in artwork that is created by international artists. The vibrancy of the place can be attributed to the beautiful art pieces that have been neatly stacked together under one roof. The best part is that there are interesting sculptures that make this gallery more attractive, one of the most prominent one being the dinosaur sculpture that is indeed quite impressive. You can learn about Abu Dhabi's culture in depth after checking out some local artworks. Etihad Modern Art Gallery is located near Al Bateen Area and can be reached easily.

Pro Tip: Good place to explore modern art

Liwa Oasis

Situated about 100 km from the south of the Persian Gulf coast in the city of Abu Dabi, the Liwa Oasis is in the Al Gharbia region. The Liwa Oasis stretches to about 100 km east-west along the arch curved towards the northern side. This oasis has some 40 villages. These villages are the southernmost settlements of the Abu Dhabi and the United Arab Emirates. When here at the Liwa, you can carry out a range of activities to keep yourself entertained. Get out into the desert, and you have great opportunities to have a fun family picnic time away from home. Camping here in the Liwa Oasis is also an ideal way to have an exciting weekend gateway.

Historical Context: The Liwa Oasis is the birth place of the ruling families of the Abu Dhabi in Dubai.

Pro Tip: To get around the Liwa oasis you must have your own vehicle. Of course there is some hitchhiking but you can't rely on it.

Al Lulu Island

Al Lulu or simply the Lulu Island is an idyllic looking island that comprises of the dunes, sandy beaches, and the date palms. These are visible from the Corniche, and the island is just a short boat ride away from the Marina on the Breakwaters. The island has risen like a mirage from the sea as one of the most ambitious tourist projects of the Abu Dhabi city. Lulu has not yet been opened to the public, however, in order to explore the island well you can take a boat ride and enjoy the serenity and calmness of the island. Until the time the island is open for public access, you should enjoy the attraction on the boat.

Historical Context: Al Lulu has officially been shut down for the public however it can be accessed via private boat only.

Qasr Al-Hosn

The Al Hosn Palace is also known as the White Fort or the Old Fort. It is the oldest building in Abu Dhabi and was built in the year 1793 so as to offer residence to the ruling family as well as the seat of the government. The interiors of this monument have been modernized and renovated and are today used by the Cultural Foundation for the purpose of research and documentation. Here there is a huge collection of documents relating to the history and heritage of the Gulf region and the United Arab Emirates. Some of the notable features of this palace are the courtyard and the beautiful tile work on the main northern gate of the fort. It is a great medium to transport yourself to the history of emirates.

Historical Context: It was constructed in the year 1761 as a colonial watchtower with an object of defending the only freshwater well in Abu Dhabi island.

Pro Tip: Visit during the Qasr Al Hosn Festival that is conducted anually.

Aldar HQ Building

Aldar HQ Building is one of the famous modern manmade structures that are present in UAE. This is a shell-shaped building that is made in an interesting manner. A number of engineers and architects have acknowledged this structure that is simply exquisite. In order to reach Aldar HQ Building, you need to travel 20 km away from the main city. Public transport in this area is limited so prefer traveling in a cab. The structure is primarily known for its architectural exquisiteness and is the reason it's buzzing with tourist activity on a usual day. The view of the building only gets better in the evening, when the rays of the setting sun light up the building.

Pro Tip: The architecture of this place is exquisite

St. Joseph's Cathedral

St. Joseph's Cathedral is located in Abu Dhabi City. You will admire the decent architecture of the church building. Once you enter the premises, the first thing you notice is the stone walls. Not just Catholics, people from all religions visit St. Joseph's Cathedral to seek blessings of the Lord. St. Joseph's Cathedral is a wonderful religious destination that is open for all. You can hire a guide in order to learn about the history of this place. The evening mass at St. Joseph's Cathedral should be attended if you are planning to pay a visit. Two beautiful sculptures of Mother Mary and Jesus Christ welcome you in the church. Make sure you do not make any noise when inside the church.

Pro Tip: Parking space might be a mess

Ferrari World

The financial capital of United Arab Emirates is Abu Dhabi. It is one of the most resplendent as well as opulent cities in the world. One of the greatest attractions in the city is the Yas Island that is known to be the epicenter of the best entertainment and the greatest sightseeing in Abu Dhabi. In the year 2010, Ferrari World Abu Dhabi came into being. It is a fully air-conditioned amusement park that is covered by the 200,000 square meters red roof, making it the largest theme park in the world. The park was labeled the "Middle East's Leading Tourist Attraction." When you enter the beautiful park, you'll be greeted by a line of revving up engines of the Ferrari.

Historical Context: It has been lauded with the World Travel Awards 2015.
Pro Tip: Try the world's fastest roller coaster here.

Aldar HQ Building

Aldar HQ Building is one of the famous modern manmade structures that are present in UAE. This is a shell-shaped building that is made in an interesting manner. A number of engineers and architects have acknowledged this structure that is simply exquisite. In order to reach

Aldar HQ Building, you need to travel 20 km away from the main city. Public transport in this area is limited so prefer traveling in a cab. The structure is primarily known for its architectural exquisiteness and is the reason it's buzzing with tourist activity on a usual day. The view of the building only gets better in the evening, when the rays of the setting sun light up the building.

Pro Tip: The architecture of this place is exquisite

Mushrif Central Park

Spend some time in green surroundings, away from the hustle bustle of the concrete jungle at the Mushrif Central Park. Loved by adults and children alike, a visitor can also explore the animal barn in the close vicinity of the park. There is a huge open space at the park open to the public where one can indulge in a number of recreational activities. You will find many kids playing in the playground at any time of the day. While it's a great place to visit during most hours of the day, mornings and evenings are usually people's favorite. There are a number of water features in the park that makes the whole ambiance look attractive. You can plan a picnic at Mushrif Central Park on weekends with family and folks.

Pro Tip: Best place for family picnics

Al Maqta'a Fort

Al Maqtaa Fort is a lovely piece of work of renowned architects that has been a jewel in Abu Dhabi's crown for a long time now. Take a boat to visit this monument, which is both attractive and subtle in terms of its design. It's best you hire a guide to take you through the important pages of Abu Dhabi's history and how this structure is relevant to it. The area around the fort is beautiful and picturesque, especially in the evenings. The Al Maqta Bridge close to the fort is the perfect place to enjoy the view of the sunset. A number of tourists visit this landmark so as to click pictures, enjoy the pleasant view, and soak in the beauty of this gorgeous destination.

Pro Tip: Do hire a guide to visit this place

Green Mubazzarah

Green Mubazzarah is a unique place that is admired by the locals in Abu Dhabi. This is a lovely destination that offers a relaxed time to the visitors. The green area at Green Mubazzarah is quite fascinating in the middle of the dessert. There is a natural hot spring water source that is active on the premises. The tourist population loves visiting Green Mubazzarah due to its excellent setup. Activities such as horse riding are also offered at Green Mubazzarah that keeps the visitors interested. If you wish to spend a lovely time away from the city noise, then do visit this location to spend a quiet holiday with friends and family members. The evening time is perfect to walk on the grass and enjoy the sunset view.

Pro Tip: Do splash into the hot spring water

Abu Dhabi Mar Thoma Church

Abu Dhabi Mar Thoma Church is active in the city that works to harmonize divinity among the people. This church is working since many years to help the needy people. The prayer meetings held at this church are quite rejuvenating. Abu Dhabi Mar Thoma Church has a melodious choir that makes the whole ambience soothing with the songs of the Lord. You will surely love this religious landmark that is present close to the Industrial Area in Abu Dhabi. Visit the church with your family or loved one to seek the blessings of god in a calm state. You can reach Abu Dhabi Mar Thoma Church using public transport.

Pro Tip: Do not attend the choir sessions

Murjan Splash Park

Murjan Splash Park will surely keep you entertained. There are very few destinations in Abu Dhabi that attract a lot of public and this water park is one of them. There are slide rides which are designed in order to keep the public happy. Murjan Splash Park is a good place for kids. There are separate rides that are designed for little ones. The summer season is perfect to visit this place that is full of excitement and fun. The ticket prices are quite attractive, and you can access a number of food items at Murjan Splash Park. Safety gears are offered to the public so that they can enjoy their rides at ease.

Pro Tip: Interesting rides that are totally safe

MusicHall

The Music Hall is a wonderful place to enjoy the interesting shows that include music, dance, and drama. This place can be reached easily via public transport. The atmosphere is very vibrant, which is loved by the crowd. The best time to access a show at The Music Hall is in the evening. The Music Hall is managed in a wonderful manner that makes it a good destination to watch cultural as well as artist performances. The food offered at The Music Hall is decent while the parking space might create a mess on the weekends. Make sure you book your show tickets in advance so as to avoid any hassle. The Music Hall is a good spot for creative people who wish to stay entertained.

Pro Tip: Carry a city map to reach this place

Al Bateen Beach

Al Bateen Beach is a beautiful beach that is situated towards the west of the Abu Dhabi. It has uninterrupted scenic views and the clear waters that are extremely popular among the UAE locals for the fishing, waterfront picnics, and swimming. The beach has recently been lauded with the Blue Flag sustainability award by the Wildlife Authority of Emirates. Covering some 800 meters of the pristine waterfront, the beach has available amenities such as changing rooms, children playgrounds as well as the toilets. Anyone who is on a lookout for some action, fun, and thrill in Abu Dhabi, The Al Bateen Beach is simply ideal. You can play beach volleyball or just enjoy some water sports like paddling, kayaking, etc.

Pro Tip: Engage yourself in an interesting match of volleyball on the beach.

Emirates Park Zoo

Emirates Park Zoo is a prominent zoo in the Abu Dhabi that has a host of animals at its wildlife park. Some of the most notable animals found at the zoo include the elephants, rare and exotic white tigers and the giraffes. There is a dedicated section of the zoo where one can come across the different types of monkeys. Almost every breed of monkey found anywhere in the world can be found at this park. There is also a flamingo park with a sea lion enclosure. At the Emirates Park Zoo, you not only view these multi-species animals and birds but also get up and close with them. Yes, you can touch them, feed them and even click pictures with them.

Pro Tip: Don't forget to click pictures with elephants or giraffes here.

Folklore Gallery

Another art gallery that showcases the classic works of local artists is the Folklore Gallery. This place is visited by art lovers who wish to delve deeper into the culture of Abu Dhabi. This art gallery is not that vast but will surely impress you. Make sure you visit this place in the afternoon time. Folklore Gallery should be visited with a guide who will help to offer detailed information about all the items present in this space. Make sure you do not touch anything in the museum as it is strictly prohibited. Do carry eatables inside the gallery. Artistically arranged and aesthetically designed, Folklore Gallery is a great choice for visit when holidaying in Abu Dhabi.

Pro Tip: Excellent place to check out local art work

Al Ain Zoo

Al Ain Zoo is a huge 400-hectare zoo that is located in the foothills of the Jabel Hafeel Mountains in the United Arab Emirates. The zoo comprises of the Arabian antelopes, lechwe, gazelle, oryz as well as the eland that can be found in the tree-shaded paddocks. All the birds and the animals residing here get phenomenal breeding conditions and are given a safe environment to live, breathe, and grow. At the Al Ain Zoo, one can see the almost extinct white lion. There are not more than 200 white lions remaining in the world. It also features a great range of big cat house, jaguars, lions, pumas and the leopards. To browse through these and to explore the zoo at best, you must take a safari ride here.

Pro Tip: Do carry food along with you.

Emirates Palace

Emirates Palace is a luxurious hotel in the city that should be visited. This destination is located close to Etihad Towers and can be reached easily using public transport. The cappuccino served at Emirates Palace in the evening is very popular among the visitors who have stayed at this landmark. An architectural marvel, the heritage property is managed in the best of forms. This place is accessed for business meetings and get-togethers by the local as well as tourist crowd. The staff working at Emirates Palace is very helpful and efficient that offers a comfortable stay to people who book the property. The five-star restaurant at Emirates Palace is known for its ultimate cuisine that includes local dishes along with international recipes.

Pro Tip: The interior of the hotel is marvelous

Arabian Wildlife Park

In the year 1971, Sir Bani Yas Island was recognized as a natural reserve by the late UAE President Sheikh Zayed bin Sultan Al Nahyan. He recognized the very need to preserve the animals that were on the verge of extinction particularly in the Arabian Peninsula and the UAE.

It was his vision that led to the establishment of the Arabian Wildlife Park. The park covers just about half of the island and assisted in the rehabilitation as well as the breeding of the animals and the birds. Spread over an area of 1400 hectares of land, the park is a home to a variety of members from the animal kingdom, be it the cheeky Ostrich or the graceful Giraffe- you can find it all here. A visit to the park is a great experience for wildlife enthusiasts and nature lovers who want to explore the flora and fauna of a place.

About Saadiyat Beach

The Saadiyat Public Beach brings forth an ideal setting for an everyday retreat. Set on the natural shores of the island, this 400-meter beach is indeed a great spot for an ideal day out with family. Here at the beach, you can enjoy the clean and warm turquoise waters of the beach. Facilities such as showers, lockers, umbrellas, chairs, bathrooms, changing rooms, lifeguards, ample parking space and the towels are available for easy access all throughout the day. You can either swim in the clean waters of the beach or take a romantic stroll on the white sandy shoreline of the beach. When you get tired from all the fun activities at the beach, you can sit back and munch on some beach snacks.

Pro Tip: You can take swimming equipments and gears from the shops on the beach

Manarat Al Saadiyat

Manarat Al Saadiyat is a hub of cultural as well as artistic activities that take place in the city. The place is sure to entice you with its antics and keep you wanting for a lot more. Louvre Abu Dhabi will soon be built in the same area. Zayed National Museum along with other exhibitions is present in Manarat Al Saadiyat. Over the year, conferences, workshops, and performances are active in this area. You need not miss a chance to visit Manarat Al Saadiyat with your friends and family to explore the true beauty of the city. There is also a gift shop and library present in the area that can also be accessed by the public.

Historical Context: The main galleries of Manarat Al Saadiyat are dedicated to exhibitions and educational programmes which are organized by Abu Dhabi Tourism & Culture Authority

Pro Tip: The performances in this area shouldn't be missed

Sheikh Zayed Bridge

The Sheikh Zayed Bridge is an arch bridge in the city of Abu Dhabi in the United Arab Emirates. It is approximately 842 meters long and has been named after the country's chief architect and the president, Sheikh Zayed bin Sultan Al Nahyan as a grandeur landmark of the city. Intricately designed, the curved design of the bridge evokes undulating sand dunes of the nearby dessert. Besides being architecturally rich, the bridge has a dynamic lighting design that brings forth the subtle colors that flow past the spine of the bridge. In a way, the Sheikh Zayed Bridge symbolizes the energy and the connecting nature of the city that the Abu Dhabi city radiates. To marvel at the architecture of the Bridge, you must visit it once.

Historical Context: Sheikh Zayed Bridge is conceived in an open setting and has due prospects of becoming a destination in itself and will thereby act as a potential catalyst in the future urban growth of the city.

Fun City

Fun City is an amusement park for kids aged between 1-12 years. There are rides that are safely planned so that the little ones can enjoy their trip to this interesting destination. There are all sorts of rides in this area ranging from bumper cars, ships, and even roller coasters. Your child will love the time at Fun City, and you can relax since the amusement park is known to be one of the safest in the city. The area is well planned and has food stalls that offer delicious snacks. You need time in order to explore this place with your kids. The best time to visit this place is on weekdays as the weekends are very crowded.

Historical Context: Fun City was established in 1999
Pro Tip: Tak taxi to reach this destination

Warehouse421

Warehouse421 is a great place for art connoisseurs. This area is managed in a classic way so as to offer a wonderful view of the various art works. A new art museum gaining popularity in the city, Warehouse421 has interesting sculptures along with media displays that make the place look vibrant. It is a cultural space that encourages artists to showcase their talent. The area consists of food stalls and live entertainment that keep the crowd happy. Plan a visit on the weekdays to avoid the rush. The place is known for its exquisite interiors that are also a unique point of interest about the place. Once inside, make sure you don't touch anything.

Historical Context: It was opened for public in 2015
Pro Tip: Do not touch anything in the museum

Fujairah

The Emirate of Fujairah is unique among the rest of the Emirates, because it is located on the Gulf of Oman, outside the Strait of Hormuz. The beaches of Fujairah extend on about 90 Kilometers along the Gulf of Oman, which gives Fujairah its unique and important strategic location.

The area of the Emirate Fujairah is 1165 square kilometers, equivalent to 1.5% of the total area of the country, without the islands. The total population is 125,698 people, according to the census of December 2005. Fujairah City is the capital of the Emirate of Fujairah, and the residence of His Highness Sheikh Hamad Bin Mohammed Al-Sharqi, the Ruler, and the place of all government departments, institutions and commercial companies.

The City of Fujairah also includes The port of Fujairah, which greatly helped in stimulating Shipping activities and trade, as well as Fujairah International Airport. Fujairah is famous for the existence of a series of rugged mountains that are trapped between Fujairah and the Eastern Coast of the Gulf of Oman, which is one of the most fertile regions of the country, and it is full of farms.

Fujairah is characterized by viable tourist beaches on the coastline, and adjacent high mountains in many areas of the sea shore, natural valleys and springs of marvelous scenes. Dibba is one of the important areas of Fujairah, which is famous for fishing, besides including many projects of agriculture and livestock.

The Heritage village of Fujairah is located next to Ain Madab park, where it features the perception of the ancient past with all its characteristics and specifications, such as old houses, ancient food-cooking war, that was used by our ancestors, as well as methods of old irrigation of farms. The Museum of Fujairah showcases archaeological and cultural materials, that have been discovered in the Emirate of Fujaira, and date back to 4500 years ago, in addition to Al Badiya Mosque, which is one of the oldest mosques in the United Arab Emirates, it is known as the Mosque of Othman, and it is famous for the unique design of the four small domes at the top surface of the Mosque.

Sights

Travelling to UAE usually means a trip to Dubai or Abu Dhabi. However, there is an Arabic city which is set apart from the usual glitzy, contemporary cities – a toned down town of Fujairah which is set on the eastern coast along the Gulf of Oman and bordered by the rugged Hajar Mountains on the other side. Fujairah sets itself apart from the rest of the Emiratis which are predominantly desert lands, where as this Arabic city is mainly mountainous and has a vast coastline that levels down to pristine beaches. Relatively laid back having a population that is vaguely just a fraction of its neighbouring Emirates, Fujairah is a refreshing break and a favourite weekend escape for the Emirati locals. The city is famous for its stunning restored historical monuments, its jagged mountains and wadis, and a long stretch of clear beaches lapped up by crystal waters of Gulf of Oman. A perfect deviation to relax after a thrilling visit to fast paced cities of Dubai and Abu Dhabi, here's what you should visit when you are in Fujairah.

Al-Bidyah Mosque

Fujairah is home to the oldest mosque in UAE – the Al-Bidyah Mosque. Built of stone and mud bricks, the creation of the mosque dates to past centuries where no materials were used for making structures other than mud and stones available in the surrounding areas and is considered an accomplishment for the architecture in which it was designed. The main prayer hall has arches with a central pillar that divides the space into four sections each with domed ceilings and has number of small decorative windows that allow light and air to enter the mosque. Also known as the Ottoman Mosque, this holy shrine is functional, performing daily prayers and holds a major significance in history. The mosque's peaceful ambience is worth the visit.

Fujairah Fort

Another oldest historical monument in UAE – the Fujairah Fort takes you into the past revealing the legacy of its ruling family and the city's era being a defensive base. Perched on a hill top surrounded by lush date gardens, this fort is a wonderful structure comprising of three major sections, one square tower, two round towers, and several halls. One of the area's prime attractions, the fort holds an imprint of the city's historic significance. The nearby Heritage village gives you a glimpse through its restored houses and exhibits about the traditional lifestyle and methods of living of past Emirati inhabitants.

Ain al-Madhab Hot Springs

Fujairah has fascinating geographical elements with a mountainous terrain and beautiful beaches that makes it different from the other cities of UAE. One remarkable aspect is its picturesque hot springs set at the foot of Hajar Mountains. The Ain Al Madhad Hot Springs is a great retreat to enjoy a refreshing soak in hot pools, quite popular among tourists and a favourite family weekend spot for the locals. The mineral springs here produce warm sulphuric water that is pumped into two swimming pools making separate bathing areas for males and females. This is an amazing natural spot to just relax among Fujairah's natural surroundings.

Fujairah Beaches

The only Emirati to face the turquoise Gulf of Oman waters, Fujairah is blessed with a perfect setting of a spectacular coastline stretch. The neat beaches with crisp sand and inviting warm waters attracts tourists from all over the world and is a great place to experience loads of water activities such as swimming, surfing, yachting and much more. The clear waters rich with aquatic life and untouched reefs makes it a happening spot for underwater exploration, so gear up and venture into the waters for some close encounters amid the mesmerizing ocean life with snorkelling and scuba diving opportunities. Those who just want to have a sun soaked lazy day can wander around and enjoy the beach with plenty of recreational and dining facilities.

Masafi Market

A sober village with beautiful natural springs located on the edge of Hajar mountains is quite famous for its markets, especially Masafi Friday markets or as it is locally called 'Souq al Juma'. The town market that lies on the Dubai-Fujairah route is the best place to buy numerous handmade crafts from the locals as well as neighbouring cities and countries. The fabulous local market welcomes you with a range of attractive antiques, carpets, earthenware, and local handicrafts. Here you can stop enroute your drive and shop for indigenous and good quality articles at much cheaper rates than the high end outlets elsewhere and also take advantage to shop at bargain prices.

Wadi Wurayah National Park
With a splendid variety of topographical variations, Fujairah has a refreshing flora and fauna that is unlike any other Emirate city. Wadi Wurayah is a rare protected site and a haven for wildlife in the Middle East, filled with number of endangered species and stunning natural beauty. Located at the magnificent Hajar Mountains, a coastal road takes you to this exceptional national park through splendid surroundings of seaside and mountain views along the way. An ideal place for nature lovers, the retreat is home to some of the rarest animals in the world; you can spot several bird species, Blanford's fox, Arabian leopards, mountain gazelles, caracals and the extremely rare Arabian tahr. This hidden gem of nature at the Hajar mountains with

breathtaking scenery is a refreshing excursion not to be missed while visiting Fujairah.

Sheikh Zayed Mosque

One of the largest mosques across the UAE, The brand new Sheikh Zayad Mosque is a marvellous structure fusing contemporary and traditional designs and is one of the major landmarks of the city. Built on a grand scale, the mosque occupies an area that can cover three football pitches and is constructed with high minarets, series of small domes and a huge domed prayer hall all made up of white granite and marble. The newest addition to Fujairah's lists of amazing attractions, this grand edifice is a sight to marvel and a must visit on your journey.

With a beautifully sun soaked stretch of immense coastline that is ideal for many water sports, a great mountainous landscape of Hajar mountains that allures adventurers, rich historical structures with unique architecture and a peacefully paced lifestyle all add up to Fujairah being a destination that breaks away from the usual sophisticated travel spaces in the Emirates and makes it an experience worth cherishing. In fact, several tourists, who travel to Dubai, often drive to Fujairah to relax as it is only 40 minutes drive from Dubai. So next time you are in the Emirates, take a detour to Fujairah for an entirely different idyllic experience.

Best Things to Do in Fujairah

Sat on a different body of water, backed by mountains rather than desert and with a population less than one tenth of Abu Dhabi's, Fujairah can seem a world away from the rest of the UAE and in many ways, it is. But it is a world just three hours' drive away and there is lots to explore for trip happy Abu Dhabians. Check off *Time Out* Abu Dhabi's list of 20 places that need to go on your Fujairah travel itinerary.

Diving and snorkelling:

While Abu Dhabi diving is good for exploring reef systems, the Fujairah coast, especially north towards Khor Fakkan and Dibba, has more sea life. Either with an organised dive or simply snorkelling it is not unusual to see turtles, sharks and rays among enormous schools of fish. Most Fujairah hotels offer diving packages in the Indian Ocean. Alternatively, dive specialist Al Boom has a dive centre at Le Meridien Al Aqah Beach Resort. Al Boom offers equipment hire and guided dives at the best spots.

Al Boom Diving Centre, Le Meridien Al Aqah, Fujairah, (09 204 4925).

Wadis and mountains:

Drag your eyes away from the Indian Ocean and look back inland for views of the imposing Hajar Mountain backdrop. The craggy mountains and wadis offer the country's best hiking spots and some amazing scenery. Different to the rolling dunes and pristine beaches, this is rugged and challenging. Until you know the area better, hiking and mountain biking should be done with an organised tour group – especially as we've heard reports of currently popular areas such as Wadi al-Wuraya being closed off in recent months. Tour organiser Absolute Adventure has hiking and cycling tours for all ability levels, including a Dibba Mountain trek and coastal tour.

Dibba Climb Dhs350 for adults, Dhs350 for kids. Absolute Adventure, 606 SIT Tower, Silicon Oasis, Dubai, (04 392 6463).

Bull-butting and a Friday Market:

You won't get a better feel of the difference between East and West coast than by combining a trip to the Masafi Friday Market (we know that it's technically Ras Al Khaimah but it is just 20 minutes from Fujairah) and an iconic Fujairah sport. Driving on the E88, you will suddenly come to the Friday Market in Masafi about 30km before Fujairah centre. Stop and take in the sights, sounds and smells and pick out bargain rugs, ceramics and fresh fruit and vegetables. After stocking up, continue on to Fujairah to see some bull-butting. Every Friday on Fujairah corniche, on an open and flat stretch of dusty, bare land, hundreds of spectators gather to watch the ancient sport of bull-butting. The sport entails two enormous bulls locking horns and undertaking bouts of what is best described as 'bull sumo'. To witness this unforgettable sight, drive to the Oman end of the corniche and turn right.

Crowds start to appear at around 5pm.

Add a new mall to your collection:

Capital residents, at least, will not find anything overly groundbreaking about Fujairah's flagship shopping mall. But tourists and mall-collectors will appreciate the usual collection of more than 100 high-street stores, an impressive food court, 11-screen cinema and Magic Planet entertainment centre. The central location makes it convenient for a mid-adventure cool off and refuel as you move from mountain to beach or vice versa.

City Centre Fujairah, (09 201 2310).

Watersports and boat trips:

If scuba or snorkelling are not your scene, there is still stacks of sea-based activities to try in Fujairah and the International Marine Club is the hub for many of them. This stretch of coast has the UAE's best fishing with dorado, yellowfin tuna, sailfish, amberjacks and marlins all realistic targets. Trips are organised from the marine club or if you'd rather just sight see and pleasure ride, there are boat and jet-ski rentals offering that. If you're lucky you might also see a convoy of Harley-Davidson riders pull up at the club's Bikers Café as this is a popular end for weekend road trips.

Fujairah International Marine Club, Corniche Street, Fujairah, (09 222 1166).

Where to eat

McGettigan's Fujairah:

Just like the Abu Dhabi and Dubai branches of the ever-expanding Irish chain, only more so. With the relative lack of competition, McGettigan's has a stream of ladies' nights, open mic gigs, quiz nights, sport screenings, happy hours and brunches that make this a Fujairah favourite. Pub food staples such as burgers, pies and fish and chips are served in abundance.

Daily, noon-1am. McGettigans, Tennis & Country Club, behind Ajman University, Fujairah, (224 4880)

Waves:

The wonderful beaches are one of Fujairah's best attractions, so why not extend your beaching hours by sitting down to eat on one? The Fujairah Rotana's romantic restaurant, Waves, sits on the sands and from your candlelit table in a private cabana the views across the Indian Ocean are sublime. Our tip though, if you are here to propose, avoid the grilled seafood platter – nobody is going to say yes after watching you demolish THAT mountain of food.

Sun-Thu 7pm-10.30pm, Fri-Sat 7pm-11pm. Waves, Fujairah Rotana, Al Aqah, (09 244 9888).

Sensasia:

Despite the Miramar Al Aqah's beachfront access, this pan-Asian restaurant is an indoors affair with a dark dining room. Thankfully, it falls on the stylish end of the dark spectrum with stylish décor and dramatic Asian furnishings. Food is premium Asian with Japanese teriyaki, Indonesian nasi goreng, Chinese Manchurian and Singapore lobster among the offerings.

Daily 7pm-11pm. Sensasia, Miramar Al Aqah Beach Resort, Al Aqah, Fujairah, (09 244 9994).

Sardinia:

Authentic Italian cuisine from the kitchens of Italian chef Angelo Usai have given this restaurant quite the buzz in Fujairah. The dining room is simplistic and the location next to free zone gates makes it a less obvious choice when compared to some of the more glamorous hotels, but ask diners exiting the restaurant if they enjoyed the genuine Italian food made the traditional way and the answer is likely to be a resounding yes. A gem in Fujairah.

Daily 12.30pm-3.30pm, 7.30pm-11.30pm. Sensasia, The Club, Sakamkam, Fujairah (228 3601).

Al Meshwar:

A visit to this enormous Lebanese eatery is nothing if not an experience. From the outside it looks like a cross between a castle and a mountain (perhaps a nod to the surrounding forts and hills) while the cavernous inside has moons and stars painted onto ceilings. Try and order if you like but it's better to hand over decision making to the legion of waiters who scurry between tables dropping off grilled meat

platters, hot breads and piles of hot and cold mezze along the way.
Al Meshwar, Hamad Bin Abdullah Road, Fujairah (09 222 1113).

What to see
Al Badiyah Mosque

In a country short on historic attractions the nation's oldest mosque is a standout sight. Believed to be more than 500-years-old and still hosting daily prayers, the mud and stone built mosque was awarded a Certificate of Excellence. A must to see the region's history.

To arrive at the mosque take the coastal road north out of Fujairah and past Khor Fakkan until reaching the village of Badiyah.

Fujairah Fort
This fantastic old fort outdates the formation of the UAE by centuries and has a colourful and proud history. Damaged in the early twentieth century by British soldiers it has since been restored to its former glory and the surrounding area turned into a heritage village that should sit high on your list of must-see sites both night and day.
Fujairah Museum, Fujairah Heritage Village (09 222 9085).

Fujairah Museum:

While Fujairah Fort rightly dominates holiday photo albums, the neighbouring museum (part of a Heritage Village attraction) is worthy of exploration. Artefacts lay claim to more than 3,000 years of settlements in the region and there is the usual Bedouin museum displays of tools, jewels and weapons from historic tribes in the area. *Fujairah Museum, Fujairah Heritage Village (09 222 9085).*

Al Hayl Castle:

Drive 15 minutes out of Fujairah and there is another excellent historic attraction. Al Hayl Castle is believed to have been built in around 1830 and is one of the best preserved buildings from that era. You can only access it by a slim dirt track, but if you have a 4x4 the potential photos alone make it worth the trip. Except on Fridays there is usually somebody around to give you a mini tour of the stunning fort and surrounding archaeological areas.

Take the E89 from near the City Centre Mall and follow the signposts southwest out of Fujairah for approx. 13km.

Al Bithnah Fort:

The third genuine must-see military fort in Fujairah is believed to be an 18th century landmark and has played a role in the East Coast's colourful military history. A watch point across the hajar mountains, it is also one of the first attractions you can see from the Masafi road into Fujairah. No matter how keen you are to get to your hotel and beach, no weekend in Fujairah photo album is complete without stopping off for a picnic here. Follow the E89 out of Masafi for 16km towards Fujairah until you pass through the village of Bithnah and see the fort on the right hand side.

Where to stay

Le Meridien Al Aqah:

Le Meridien Al Aqah combines the quality service and facilities of a premium Abu Dhabi hotel with a secluded location to make for great getaways of the sporting, romantic or family type. It has 230m of private beach, a highly regarded spa, watersports kids and teen clubs and good dining options. A sparkling Friday brunch is held at Views (Dhs200 if booked online) but if you prefer to keep the day free for exploration then an evening meal at Thai restaurant Taste before a visit to top floor grape bar Astros, is recommended. Regular deals and packages for weekend trippers are offered although promotions are currently transitioning from summer to Autumn, so check ahead for details.

Standard room from Dhs650. Le Meridien Al Aqah, Dibba Road, Fujairah, (09 244 9000).

Sandy Beach Hotel:

This low-rise beach resort has been attracting divers to its shores for decades. The main attraction is 'Snoopy Rock' just a short swim from the private beach. Named after its uncanny resemblance to the sleeping cartoon dog it is a great snorkelling and Scuba diving spot. The arrival of big name hospitality neighbours has led to a major refurbishment in recent years. Rooms and chalets that were once 'surfer chic' are now modern and comfortable. Dining is still limited but the addition of Amouage, a beach shack-themed seafood restaurant now means there is onsite food worth staying around for, which was not always the case.

Beach chalet from Dhs400 per night. Sandy Beach Hotel, Dibba Road, Fujairah, (09 244 5555).

Hilton Fujairah:
The centrally located Hilton Fujairah is close to the city centre so offers easy access to heritage, shopping and basic nightlife attractions making it more suitable if you're making the hotel a hub rather than a final destination. Having said that, it does have an impressive stretch of beach, and water sports and a tennis court are on hand if you're done with exploring for the day. Buffet restaurant Al Ghorfa has different theme nights every day of the week and is on a par with a decent Abu Dhabi buffet. Fez nightclub is unlikely to attract the big name DJs you see in Dubai but its late bar, live band and pool tables will keep you entertained until 3am.

From Dh695 per night. Hilton Fujairah, E99, Fujairah, www.hilton.com (09 222 2411).

Novotel Fujairah:
Sacrifice direct beach access and you make a big saving on price in Fujairah and with rooms at less than Dhs300, the Novotel is worth considering. Located amid a cluster of hotels it is just minutes away from the Fujairah City Centre mall. A lounger on the terrace swimming pool has good views so you can top up a tan before the sun disappears

behind the Hajar Mountains. If you're determined to stay in the hotel – and after coming such a long way it would be a shame – then the best dining option is all-day dining international restaurant, Flavours.
From Dh295 per night. Novotel Fujairah, Hamad Bin Abdullah Road, Fujairah, (09 223 9999).

Radisson Blu Resort Fujairah
Drive north approximately 50km north of Fujairah city and you will find one of the nation's most secluded beach resorts. The O2 Spa, infinity pool and long stretch of beach give it a decadent feel while the dramatic mountain meets coast location make for a beautiful setting. Other than interact with the scenery through a variety of adventurous ways, there is not a great deal to do in this small, remote corner of Fujairah. For dining options, stay on site and dine at signature Arabic seafood restaurant Al Nokhada.
From Dh500 per night. Radisson Blu Resort Fujairah, Dibba, Fujairah, (09 244 9700). All room prices quoted on booking.com for a single night on Friday September 11.

Sharjah

The Emirate of Sharjah is located on the coast of the Arabian Gulf, with a coast length of 16 km and stretches more than 80 kilometers deep inside the land. Three areas located on the East Coast of the Emirate, on the Gulf of Oman, belong to Sharjah. They are Kalba, Khor Fakkan and Dibba Al Hosn.

The area of the Emirate of Sharjah is about 2590 square kilometers, equivalent to 3.3 % of the total area of the country, without counting its islands. Its total population is 793,573 people according to the census of December 2005. The City of Sharjah is the capital of the Emirate of Sharjah. It is located on the Arabian Gulf and is the residence of His Highness Sheikh Sultan Bin Mohammed Al Qassimi, the Ruler. It also hosts all the government departments, companies, banks and hotels.

The city and its markets and commercial buildings are designed on the Islamic model. There are also many entertainment areas, such as Al Qasba Canal, the Park Island and the Corniche of Khalid Lake. The city has in particular a very large number of mosques.

Sharjah International Airport and Port Khalid are some of the important places in Sharjah. There are some oases in Sharjah; one of which is AL Dhaid, with its fertile land and a lot of farms, that produce large quantities of vegetables and agricultural products. The Eastern region of Sharjah lies on the Gulf of Oman, including Khor Fakkan, which is one of the most important cities, with its important sea port, as well as the islands of Abu Musa and Seer Bu Naeer.

The cultural and educational monuments give the Emirate of Sharjah its true image of a modern city, which is nevertheless holding its culture and traditions. The historical Museums, heritage locations and archaeological sites are evidences of the influence of that era on the modern life of Sharjah.

Sharjah was chosen by The UNESCO as the Capital of the Arab Culture for the year 1998, as a result of the tireless efforts of His Highness Sheikh Dr. Sultan bin Mohammed Al Qassimi, Supreme Council Member and Ruler of Sharjah, which made Sharjah the capital of culture on the Gulf and Arab levels. Sharjah is the home of global Nature Museums, including the Museum of Fine Arts, which contains a rare selection of historical artifacts of a significant importance to the history of the United Arab Emirates.

The unique strategic location of Sharjah in the center of the UAE helped in achieving prosperity in the International Navigation Traffic through the past 65 years. the Emirate of Sharjah stretches on the shores of the Gulf of Oman, covering vast areas of valleys and mountains. The city of Sharjah is surrounded by many hotels overlooking the beaches and Khalid Lake, supported by a number of restaurants, gardens and parks.

Best Time to Visit Sharjah

The winter months are ideal for visiting Sharjah as the summers can get very hot. The average temperature during the winters months - between October and April is 20 degrees Celsius, making it comfortable for travellers to roam the city. The temperatures drop further in the night making it extremely pleasant. Sharjah witnesses dry climate so while there is no fear of humidity, this often makes the summer months very hot with temperatures rising to 40 degrees Celsus. Travelling around the city at this time is hence very uncomfortable.

People of Sharjah

Sharjah is a conservative Islamic city and its culture and lifestyle reflect strict adherence to the tenets of Islam. Sharjah Emirate and the city is the only Emirate in the UAE that bans the sale and consumption of alcohol with a license. It also initiated strict public decency laws in 2001 that prohibits men and women who are not related by law to be seen in public, and orders a strict conservative dress code for both men and women. These rules apply to tourists as well. The weekends in Sharjah have been revised to make Friday and Saturday as holidays to respect Friday, the Muslim day of prayer. During the holy month of Ramadan, when a majority of the city's population is fasting, there are additional rules for proper public conduct.

Culture of Sharjah

Sharjah is the cultural capital of the Arab world and it has been the city's effort to showcase to the world, and its citizens, the wonders of Islamic culture, architecture, cuisine and music. It is the most religiously conservative city in the UAE and hosts a Sharia-style law with stringent rules pertaining conduct between sexes, dressing in public, and consumption and sale of alcohol. Barring these restrictions

Sharjah is an open city that has invested heavily in attracting tourism. The Heritage Area, which contains the Heritage Museum, art galleries and the covered Souk in the city with antique jewellery and clothing for sale, is one of Sharjah's biggest tourist attractions. There are an array of festivals that are hosted in Sharjah like the Islamic Arts Festival, Sharjah Light Festival, Sharjah International Arabian Horse Festival, Sharjah Heritage days, Al Qasba Food Festival, Sharjah Calligraphy Biennial, Ramadan & Summer Shopping Festival, Sharjah Water Festival and many more that offer entertainment for all.

Cities/Towns

East Coast

From sunbathing on sandy beaches to canoeing among mangroves, high mountain drives and dhow cruises on turquoise waters, the emirate of Sharjah has it all. Apart from the city of Sharjah, following are some of the most happening cities/enclaves in the emirate:

Khorfakkan

The name Khorfakkan translates to 'Creek of the Two Jaws' reflecting its setting in a splendid bay flanked on either side by headlands. This is Sharjah's largest town on the east coast, located midway between Dibba Al Hisn and Fujairah, with the focal point of the economy centred on an ever-expanding container terminal and port. A long stretch of sandy beach backed by a promenade runs alongside the bay and is a pleasant place to wander.

Set in the mountains above the town is the Al Rifaisa Dam – a holding area to contain floodwater and to serve the settlements below.

Wadi Wurrayah is a popular and beautiful natural site located some 15 kilometres inland from Khorfakkan. Accessible by 4WD, the wadi features a deep year round pool with a seasonal waterfall.

Kalba

Kalba retains its historical charm with fascinating old forts and a museum to explore. It is the UAE's most south east settlement before the border with Oman.

Khor Kalba: The tidal creek just south of Kalba, the southernmost tip of the UAE's Gulf of Oman coastline is the site of the oldest mangrove forest of Arabia and is an important conservation site for endangered species. This tranquil and beautiful landscape with its dark green mangroves is inhabited by two of the world's rarest birds: the White-Collared Kingfisher and Syke's Warbler.

Tourist flock to Kalba in particular for bird watching, kayaking and hiking trips along nature trails. This is a great family holiday destination with plenty of outdoor activities on offer.

Dibba

Dibba is a sleepy set of three seaside villages belonging to the Sultanate of Oman (Dibba Bayah), Fujairah (Dibba Muhallab) and in between the two, Sharjah (Dibba Al Hisn). These fishing communities share a beautiful bay and it is worth visiting the harbours in the late afternoon to see the daily catch. Green palms, the old fort and brightly painted metal doorways bring character and colour to this attractive area.

Famous for its Islamic history, Dibba was the site of one of the great battles of the Ridda Wars, the reconquest of Arabia by Muslim armies in the generation after the death of the Prophet Mohammed (Peace be Upon Him). A vast cemetery on the outskirts of Dibba marks the battle site of 633 when over 10,000 rebels died.

At Dibba the mountains rise to an impressive 2,000 metres into the Mussandam Peninsula. This is a superb area for hiking trips and following nature trails.

Central Region

Al Dhaid

Al Dhaid, the peaceful palm oasis in the centre of the emirate is the third largest town and a main producer of fruit and vegetables sold in the UAE, specialising in strawberries, dates, limes, guava and mangoes.

Nearby, the impressive hilly outcrop of Fossil Rock rises up through the red sand dunes and is a popular area for dune driving, quad biking (available for hire), fossil hunting and camping.

The Camel Race Track located on the road to Meliha holds races in the winter months, usually early in the morning on Thursdays and Fridays.

Just before Masafi is the Friday Market, which contrary to its name is open every day. The market sells a variety of goods including local pottery, carpets, plants, dried fish, toys, fruit and vegetables. Prices are competitive and bargaining is expected.

Al Badayer

Located in the higher ground of Al Madam, Al Badayer is one of the most popular desert areas in the emirate of Sharjah, attracting visitors of all ages and offering scenic camping sites and challenging desert drives for 4WD vehicles and off-road bikers.

The area of Al Badayer has recently witnessed tremendous development, and is evolving into a major tourist destination.

Traditions

The time-honored traditions of the region date back to the desert tribes and the influence brought upon them by migration. These traditions have been passed on through generations by word of mouth and today are an integral part of modern Arabian lifestyle. Traditional customs and values continue to preserve and maintain family and social relationships and interactions.

Sharjah's culture is firmly rooted in the Islamic traditions of Arabia. Islam is more than a religion; it touches all aspects of everyday life and lies at the heart of Sharjah's living heritage. The values of Islam include honesty, courtesy and hospitality, attributes that visitors will be charmed by during their stay.

National Men's Attire

Comfortable and modest clothing has developed to suit the climate and lifestyle. The distinguished men's dress is the white dishdasha, a long robe or kaftan usually made from cotton or silk mixed with synthetic fibres and always immaculately pressed. Men's headgear consists of three parts; the square shaped head cloth (ghuttrah) typically white in colour, a skull cap (gahfiya) worn under the head cloth and the head circlet or agaal, a twisted woollen braid used to hold the head cloth in place.

On special occasions, an outer cloak (*Al Bisht*) of a fine wool or cotton material, with gold and sometimes silver embroidered edges, is worn over the *dishdasha*. The black Al Bisht is worn at night, rather like a dinner jacket.

National Women's Dress

A light chiffon headscarf or sheyla is worn to cover the hair but in past times the abayaor black cloak draped the entire body from head to toe. Once a fairly plain and silk covering, the crepe or chiffon abaya of today often comes richly decorated with sequins, crystals, embroidery etc.

The headgear is considered to be the most distinctive element of a woman's attire distinguishing her origins from one region to another. The traditional mask worn in the Emirates is the burqa that covers the brow, cheekbones and nose.

Arabian Gulf Cuisine

In the past, the cuisine of the Arabian Gulf countries was dominated by the simple Bedouin and pearl diver's food. Breakfast consisted of bread and pancakes, with locally caught fish or meat for lunch and dinner, served on a bed of rice. Rice was imported from the east and delivered by *dhow*. On special occasions a sheep or a goat would be killed and roasted for a feast. All year round, highly nutritious dates, either fresh or dried, would accompany most meals. In time, a wide variety of imported food and cooking methods were brought to the region, along with the aromatic spices of the East. Popular dishes today are *machbous* (a meat and rice speciality seasoned with spices, tomatoes, onions and dried lemon), *khouzi* (roasted lamb stuffed with nuts and spices), *harees* (a mixture of lamb and wheat), and *al threed* (a bread, meat and gravy dish). Arabic hospitality and traditions endure to ensure that visitors always feast in comfort.

Pastries & Sweets

As with the savoury dishes, there are many different delicious desserts. Common ingredients include margarine, sugar, cinnamon, honey, dates and nuts. Among the most famous UAE pastries are *Al Khabesa* (flour, water, sugar and saffron mix), *Al Khanfaroush* (made from flour, water, sugar and eggs), *Al Mohammar Beldebs* (white rice cooked until it turns red), Al Betheeth (flour baked with margarine and dates), *Al Qurs Al Mafrouk* (a dough that is prepared and buried in the ground to bake, the earth then shaken off and the dough rubbed with margarine and sugar), *Al Mahli* (thin biscuits made with butter and eaten with eggs with sugar), Al Khameer (kneaded flour with dates and sugar), *Al Saquo* (pastry mixed with margarine, sugar and cardamom), *Bilaleet* (a cold dish of vermicelli noodles, served with a hot flat omelette), *Mamroosa, Fouqua* and *Luqaimat*. Many of the desserts are sweetened with sugar from local dates.

Music, Dance & Folklore

Ceremonial folk dances, poetry and songs from the past have become an integral part of the modern Arabian culture. These arts have been influenced by traditional customs and values, social relations and trading with regions and countries such as East Africa, Iran and India.

Arabian folk arts from this region are based on either the arts of the desert *Bedouin* (nomadic tribes) or those of seafarers.

Community spirit and tribal allegiances are reinforced at social ceremonies such as weddings and Eid, when singing, dancing and dressing up in one's finest clothing is all important. A variety of hand carved instruments such as drums, woodwind and stringed instruments, like the *rabaha* and *oud*, tambourines and brass cymbals accompany the festivities. In the past wood was a precious commodity favoured for items of ceremonial significance. Men's dances often feature the use of swords and canes, whilst women's musical gatherings reflect the importance of jewellery and domestic crafts. Songs and the simple accompaniment of the small handheld frame drum (*tar*) and tambourine (*daff*) are popular at the bride's party, whilst the vibrant drumbeat, swaying rhythms, firing of guns and festive music are part of the bridegroom's ceremonies.

Architecture

The earliest form of shelter after nomadic Bedouin tents consisted of small huts constructed solely from palm fronds or *arish*. Later, houses were made from local coral and sea stones, held in place by mortar, with mangrove poles forming the wooden roof structure. Privacy, cooling and security were of the utmost importance in the construction of forts and homes and these features controlled the design of the buildings, along with the climate and available local resources. Wind towers are a unique feature of this region, used to create air circulation and cooling within a room. The beautifully restored Heritage and Arts Areas stand tribute to the charm and practicalities of the area's traditional buildings.

Dhows

Today the word *dhow* is used for any ship made of wood. Traditionally handcrafted in wood, these vessels are working reminders of the long tradition of maritime trade in the region. Centuries ago their owners made voyages to places as far away as China and beyond. Today most of the dhows sail between the UAE, Iran, Pakistan and India, trading in a variety of goods. The most common dhow is the *Boom*, characterised by a flat stem head with a black and white painted nose. The *Sambuq* with its pointed stem head and a more rounded bow was originally used for pearling but has since been adapted for fishing. Another common design is the *Jalibout*, a stout boat with a straight, vertical stem.

Traditional Sports

Falconry is a sport in which wild falcons are trained to attack small prey and bring the prey back for the evening meal. Originally, this was a primary means of obtaining fresh meat in a barren environment. The main prey is the Houbara Bustard, but falcons also catch hares and Stone Curlew, which inhabit the gravel plains.

The Arab Thoroughbred is famous worldwide and it is believed that the first horse racing in Sharjah took place along Al Arouba Road in front of Al Hisn (Sharjah Fort). Today one can see these magnificent animals in action at Sharjah Equestrian & Racing Club.

Camels, popularly known as 'Ships of the Desert' have competed in Arabia for centuries. These ungainly creatures maintain speeds of up to 20 kilometres per hour. Attending a camel race is a memorable experience.

Culture

Sharjah, where Islamic history has strong roots, a city-state that offers unique architectural wonders to the world, where culture and knowledge are close to people's heart, won the title of the Islamic Culture Capital for 2014 at the Organisation of Islamic Countries Conference in Baku, capital of Azerbaijan.

The prestigious title of the Islamic Culture Capital for 2014 is a recognition of the emirate's powerful influence among intellectuals, and provides a boost to Sharjah's continuous support for cultural development in line with the vision of Dr Sheikh Sultan bin Mohammed Al Qasimi, Supreme Council Member and Ruler of Sharjah.

Sharjah boasts of a long and rich tradition of hosting the most important Islamic art and culture events in the world. As a leader that upholds Islamic identity through cultural and art forms, the emirate plays a key role both locally and internationally, ensuring perpetuation of Islamic expressions through its various forms of brilliance.

Sharjah is a gateway to Islamic heritage, a treasure house of learning, art and craftsmanship. Discover the magnificent facets of Arabic lifestyle and Islamic art through Sharjah's museums, traditional souqs, heritage sites and mosques.

The Capital of Islamic Culture for 2014

Sharjah was named the Capital of Islamic Culture for 2014 in recognition of its remarkable contributions in preserving, promoting and disseminating culture at local, Arab and Islamic levels, under the guidance of His Highness Sheikh Dr. Sultan Bin Mohammed Al Qasimi Member of the UAE Supreme Council and Ruler of Sharjah. The new title provides a boost to Sharjah's cultural development and comes as a tribute to the Emirate's offer of its Islamic cultural panorama, in the form of a host of cultural and Islamic events.

The new cultural achievement crowned Sharjah for its leading cultural role at local, regional, Arab and international arenas.

Among the most prominent cultural achievements in Sharjah is the 'Culture without borders' project of establishing a library in every home. Based on the directions of The Ruler, 50 books will be distributed to every local family in the Emirate. The organizing committee is headed by Her Highness SheikhaBedourBint Sultan Al Qasimi, and the aim of this projectis to promote and emphasize the importance of cultural development among the families, especially the children.

With a budget for the project of Dhs. 150 million, diverse books in the fields of religion, health, history and children's stories will be delivered to 42,000 families, until the completion of the project in 2012.

The Cultural Capital of 1998

In 1998, Sharjah was named the 'Cultural Capital of the Arab World' by UNESCO, an honour richly deserved. Sharjah has kept the spirit of its history alive by innovatively incorporating tradition into every aspect of contemporary development. The result is a vibrant, modern Emirate that simultaneously looks forward to a bright future as it looksback respectfully to its history.

The idea of the Capital of Arab Culture falls within the framework of the Cultural Capitals Program designed in 1996 and represented and promoted in an Intergovernmental committee for cultural development: the cultural aspects of development, via increased international cooperation; the participation of citizens to cultural life; and urban creative diversity.

In the 11th Summit of the ministers' regarding the cultural development in the Arab World Sharjah was selected to be the Arab cultural capital for the year 1998 by UNESCO, in appreciation of Sharjah's cultural achievements and the success the Emirate has shown in preserving its heritage. This qualified Sharjah to be chosen 'The Arab's Cultural Capital' for 1998 by the Arab League. Mr. Federico Mayor, the Director-General of UNESCO, asserted that the decision to select Sharjah as the cultural capital of the Arab World for 1998 was an auspicious one because of its importance to the region. He explained that the selection was not only based on the rich heritage of the city, but also on the kind of cultural radiance it emits and the role it plays in cultural milieu.

UNESCO & the Capital of Arab Culture

(UNESCO) is a specialized agency of the United Nations established in 1945. The short form stands for The United Nations Educational, Scientific and Cultural Organization. UNESCO pursues its objectives through five major programs: education, natural sciences, social and human sciences, culture, and communication and information. Projects sponsored by UNESCO include literacy, technical, and teacher-training programs, international science programs, the promotion of independent media and freedom of the press, regional and cultural history projects, the promotion of cultural diversity, international cooperation agreements to secure the world cultural and natural heritage (World Heritage Sites).

Sharjah: The Cultural Capital of the Arab World for 1998

On the 11th Ministers' Summit regarding cultural development in the Arab World, Sharjah was selected to be Arab Cultural Capital for the year 1998 by UNESCO, in appreciation of Sharjah's cultural achievements and the success the emirate has demonstrated in preserving its heritage. This qualified Sharjah to be chosen the 'Arab Cultural Capital for 1998' by the Arab League. Mr. Federico Mayor, the Director-General of UNESCO, asserted that the decision to select Sharjah as the cultural capital of the Arab World for 1998 was an auspicious one because of its importance to the region. He explained that the selection was not only based on the rich heritage of the city, but also on the kind of cultural radiance it emits and the role it plays in the cultural milieu.

Traditional Arts & Crafts

Sharjah has maintained cultural traditions that date back to the days of desert tribes and the influences brought about by their migration. Such skills and trades have been handed down by word of mouth and are still evident for visitors to discover and appreciate.

Pottery Jars: Discovered at every archaeological dig are earthenware jars used for storing water and grain. Today, these are still fired in man-made wood-fuelled kilns. The various shapes and sizes of the water, grain and later oil jars, are displayed in the Sharjah Heritage Museum. New locally made pots are on sale in the Plant Souk in Al Jubail.

Bridal Chests: These old Arabic chests, which are hard to come by, were made throughout the Gulf, characterized by the solid wood (usually rosewood) with inlaid brass decoration and often secret compartments. Smaller wooden chests, with carved decoration only and many compartments were made specifically for the pearling industry. Pearls would be graded and stored in the boxes according to size, along with scales and other pearling paraphernalia.

Weaving and Embroidery: In the past, girls in the family assisted in the making of their wardrobe, and traditional patterns of embroidery and dress style were handed down from mother to daughter. Arabian embroidery is a combination of rich and harmonious needlework on strong coloured textiles, characterized by a close worked, open chain stitch. Wrists, ankles and necklines are generally embroidered, often with fine gold and silver thread, and sequins added for embellishment. The trim on the trouser is made from a narrow strip of foil to create a decorative edging. These traditional crafts are still popular pastimes amongst national women.

Daggers and Knives: Even up to the middle of the last century men would complete their attire by wearing a broad, silver embroidered waist belt and *Khanjar* (dagger). The coastal dagger of the emirates (*Khanjar Sahily*) is made of silver and is highly decorated. Quite often, the *bishak* (knife) was worn instead of the dagger, particularly in the eastern area of the UAE. The carved wooden scabbard with chased and stamped silver decoration is further embellished with silver on both the wooden hilt and the iron blade.

Doors: Traditional Arabic doors from the region are unique pieces of local heritage dating back 500 years. As well as being functional, they are one of the most important forms of decorative expression to be found in the region's forts and houses. The amount and quality of the carving depends on the price of the door and therefore the status of the household.

Date Palm: In eastern Arabia alone there are over 50 different varieties of date palm, bearing many types and qualities of fruit at different times of the year. Here the natural maturation time for dates is in the summer between June and July.

Not so many years ago this precious tree was vital for survival in a land of scarcity. The fruit provided a major natural source of highly nutritious food that could be eaten (fresh, dried or drunk as a juice) all year round, and all parts of the tree were utilized in various ways; the long thin leaves were dried then woven to make mats, baskets, brushes, bags and bowls and used as roof matting for insulation; the midrib was a vital component in the construction of the *Shashah* traditional fishing boat; the trunk was hollowed out to form a mortar with the rest carved for the pestle for crushing wheat. Locally woven mats, baskets, bags and bowls are on sale in Souk Al Arsah and Souk Al Bahar.

Perfume and Incense: These are an integral part of Arab life for both men and women and are usually family run businesses. The three types of perfume and how they are mixed are a closely guarded secret. *Attar* is the oil based perfume, *bukhoor* is the fragrant burnt incense (formed by burning the wood chips) and the third is a wax sachet, which when burnt gives off a charcoal odour. You will find many perfume shops to explore in the area between Al Bourj Avenue and the Arts Area that sell oils, incense woods, perfume bottles and traditional burners made from clay, porcelain or silver.

Henna: Made from the leaves of the Lawsonia Inermis shrub, Henna has been used for centuries to enhance beauty in the Middle East and India. Traditionally, henna is used to colour hair and to decorate the palms of hands and the soles of the feet, especially for weddings and Eid celebrations. The colouring, which also contains cooling properties, will remain on the skin for several weeks before fading. In addition to Indian and Arab beauty centres, which provide this treatment, you can buy henna in Souk Al Bahar, in front of the Arts Area.

Activities

Shopping

In a city bustling with life, you can shop almost 24 hours a day and buy everything and anything from Oriental carpets to tropical fruits, gold, silver and precious stones, jewellery, gifts and handcrafted souvenirs, designer fashions, delicious Middle Eastern sweets, the latest in electronics and so much more. Whether you are looking for a piece of furniture, the latest digital camera, a gold necklace or a diamond ring, you can shop around for the perfect shape, size or colour.

Sharjah offers a treasure trove of modern malls, stylish shops and boutiques and unique souks and bazaars. The city has several separate shopping areas with busy malls, large showrooms and smaller department stores and centres, as well as exciting furniture warehouses full of artefacts and antiques, with fantastic promotions throughout the year.

Entertainment

Sharjah has become famed as a complete tourism destination - adventurous and relaxing, family-friendly and culturally fascinating and vibrant.

Museums' Visits

Sharjah has more than 20 museums and attractions for all ages and interests, as well as amazingly diverse landscapes, countless exciting sports and activities, and a busy calendar of world-class events and festivals. There are mosques, cultural venues and heritage sites. State-of-the-art shopping malls combine with traditional souks to ensure complete shopping appeal. There is fascination at every corner in Sharjah.

Organised Tours

To discover this wonderful emirate, Sharjah has many tour operators offering exciting desert and mountain safaris, as well as city tours and shopping trips. Longer excursions can be arranged including overnight camping, as well as special interest packages for fishing, diving, golf and archaeology.

Camel riding, canoe trips, sand boarding, sand skiing, dune buggy driving and excursions to other emirates are also all on offer.

Family Fun

Entertainment for the young is available in Sharjah's malls, children's centres and museums. With many different indoor and outdoor activities available, this family destination is perfect at any time of the year.

Sharjah has a number of recreational areas and boasts over 50 attractive landscaped parks such as Al Montazah park, National park, Fun Park, and Al Buheirah Corniche, where anyone can enjoy a stroll and escape from the bustle of the city. The Emirate is also notable for its numerous elegant mosques.

Al Qasba is a major cultural hub and leisure destination, providing all kinds of recreation and entertainment attractions for adults and children. It also features a 1,500 square metre exhibition space to showcase local and international cultural and educational arts. In addition, the 'Eye of the Emirates' is among the most prominent and outstanding features of Al Qasba. The 60 metre high observation wheel has 42 fully air-conditioned cubicles offering stunning views of Sharjah and Dubai.

Fun on water

Sharjah provides ideal conditions for all water sports for most of the year. Sports enthusiasts have a diversity of activities to choose from. Most of the larger hotel clubs in Sharjah offer courses, classes and coaching in various sports as well as gymnasium facilities. Also many of the parks in the city have areas dedicated to sports enthusiasts.

A popular place for jetskis and watersports is from Al Khan Lagoon to Al Mamzar Lagoon. Al Khan Beach stretches from the old village in Al Khan to Al Layyeh area and is a very popular tourist attraction.

Palm trees surround the sandy Al Corniche Beach, stretching from Sharjah Ladies Club along the coast to Coral Beach Resort. The Khalid Lagoon is a large expanse of water with a beautiful fountain in its centre. The lagoon is encased with green lawns and palm trees, offering a magnificent tourist destination.

Al Buheirah Corniche is one of the most atmospheric areas in Sharjah. Visitors enjoy walking here, around the lagoon, passing Al Montazah Park and the Central Souk. There are also a large number of restaurants around the lagoon and several coffee shops and cafés. The

Sharjah Corniche extends from Al Buheirah Corniche to Ajman Beach, passing by the fish market. It is a destination for walkers covering a considerable distance and following the creek to the coast.

Exhilarating Activities

Sharjah also hosts watersports throughout the year - lagoons, bays and creeks for wind-surfing, with designated areas for water skiing and jet skiing; mangroves for canoeing; and the East Coast for snorkeling, fishing and diving; plus the Arabian Gulf coastal shores for sailing.

Off-road Adventures

The desert has an extraordinary beauty of its own, a primal scene that is something to behold.

Desert activities include dune-bashing, quad-biking and wadi trips. The impressive rocky mountains present stunning drives amid high and rugged scenery.

Explore the popular Wadi Bih trip that extends from Dibba to the Mussandam Peninsula, cross the mountains between Manama, Masafi and the East Coast. Visit the famous Hatta Pools with its deep canyons or go further south where green and water-filled wadis can be found near Al Ain.

East Coast

The East Coast has beautiful bays lined with sandy beaches and crystal clear waters. Famous for its watersports, snorkelling, diving and relaxing, this coast creates the ideal break for a weekend or longer. The city beaches on the Arabian Gulf coast offer safe, white sand, palm tree lined beaches with clear azure seas and gently lapping waves. The most popular beaches for sunbathing are Al Khan Beach and Al Mamzar Beach.

KhorFakkan, on the East Coast, offers a beautiful beach for swimming or barbecuing along the coast where many rocky outcrops are found. There are also charming sandy beaches and areas allocated for camping.

Al Majaz Amphitheatre

Dubbed the official venue of the Sharjah Capital of Islamic Culture (SICC) 2014 Celebrations, Al Majaz open-air Roman-style amphitheater is the first in the region.

The semi-circular theater includes several terraced seating areas that can accommodate up to 4500 spectators, and a huge stage equipped with a state-of-the-art audio system. Positioned on Al Majaz Island, Khalid Lagoon with an area of 7238 square meters, the Amphitheatre is tucked between Flag Island in the north and Al Majaz Water Front in the south, and finds itself just opposite Sharjah Hilton Hotel.

It will have conference rooms and galleries, as well as a number of shops, restaurants and green areas that will surround it from all sides along with an outstanding panoramic view of the waterfront.

Elaborating on the role of the emirate, His Highness Sheikh Dr. Sultan bin Muhammad Al Qasimi said: "Sharjah, with its people, scientific edifices, cultural platforms and historical character, has given joy a different meaning embodied in the knowledge it disseminates to continue to serve as a beacon of science among nations.

"Thanks to its abundant intellectual treasures, the emirate has managed to establish its cultural and Islamic identity so as to remain a source of pride for us, as well as for Arabs and Muslims."

Sharjah's National Theatre
Founded in 1978, is one of the most celebrated theatres of the region. The organisation has won numerous local and international awards for its contribution to the local theatrical scene, and continues to play an invaluable rule in promoting local arts and culture.

Storytelling shows, reenactments of classical stories and new performances at theatres in Sharjah are designed exclusively to enable visitors to relive the traditions of the bygone era and highlight the culture and tradition of the emirate. There are shows and activities to attract all ages.

Sharjah Events
Most of the visitors and tourists travel to Sharjah to enjoy these fantastic events happening all year round. Every year, Sharjah

organizes these events to celebrate cultural festivities and to attract tourists from all corners of the world.

Main events in Sharjah
Sharjah Light Festival
A unique event designed to capture the imagination of all, as well as highlight Sharjah's distinguished landmarks and historic buildings. This breath-taking and electrifying nine-day-February event floods Sharjah with light and colour, and celebrates the art of drawing with light and combines imagery with captivating music to create an exhilarating experience.

Sharjah Government Communication Forum
This annual Government Communication Forum is organised by Sharjah Media Centre and held under the patronage of His Highness Sheikh Dr. Sultan bin Mohammed Al Qassimi, Member of the Supreme Council, Ruler of Sharjah. The Forum provides the institutions in the emirate with the latest tools and skills needed to develop governmental communication practices.

It also attempts to correct misconceptions regarding government communication and facilitates qualifying programmes for professional practitioners in the government communication sector.

Moreover, it aims to highlight the significance of government communication and enhance its position among opinion leaders, executives of governmental institutions, and officials in Sharjah.

The forum also plays a major role in drawing the to the importance of Sharjah Media Centre and its role in supporting the government of Sharjah in its communication and media objectives.

Sharjah International Show jumping championship
Held under the generous patronage of H.H. Shk. Dr. Sultan Bin Mohammed Al Qassimi, this show jumping event gets underway at Emirates Equestrian Centre (EEC) on January when Olympic medallists and the UAE's brightest show jumping stars compete for a share of a grand prize fund. Show jumping is another equestrian sport which has seen maximum progress in the Emirates within a short span of time.

Many countries take part in this prestigious event including the GCC, the Arab and foreign countries.

World Trade Week - Sharjah
Held under the generous patronage of H.H. Shk. Dr. Sultan Bin Mohammed Al Qassimi, the World Trade Week - Sharjah is an annual week long series of trade-related conferences, exhibitions, seminars and events that celebrate and promote the importance of trade to the sustainable growth of the local, regional and global economy. Providing a unique opportunity for learning from industry experts, innovators and policy makers, this even promotes investment opportunities around the world and paves the way into new markets. It also fosters cooperation between economic departments, private enterprises and governments from around the region and the world.

Additionally, It Identifies trends and opportunities in international trade while Showcasing best practices, knowledge and insights of experts and successful companies.

In its inaugural debut, World Trade Week Sharjah will become a catalytic platform for businesses to discover new opportunities and collaborate to enhance flow of trade.

Sharjah International Arabian Horse Festival
Held at Sharjah Equestrian & Racing Club under the generous patronage of H.H. Shk. Dr. Sultan Bin Mohammed Al Qassimi, Member of the Supreme Council and Ruler of Sharjah, the goal of this festival is to shed lights on the Arabian horses as an integral part of the authentic Arabian heritage and highlights their prestigious position in the Arabian culture locally, regionally and internationally. It also highlights the importance of the Arab Identity and National Heritage especially since horses formulate a big part of them; on the other hand, these events give the foreigners the chance to enrich their knowledge about the Arabian culture. This event attracts a huge number of official personalities, dignitaries, well-known celebrities and horse lovers from various nationalities - including foreigners and Arabs from all over GCC countries.

Sharjah Heritage days
Sharjah heritage days is an active annual carnival, includes many traditional events and ideas that celebrates the cultural heritage of the

people of United Arab Emirates, and highlights the beauty of the old vocabularies aiming to spread the awareness of these vocabularies to the new generation, so that they learn a lot about old days habits and values. This colorful event signifies the locals' true cultural identity, and serves as a reminder to the younger generation of their cultural identity, the pride of their forefathers, and the foundation of what they stand for as emaratis.

Al Qasba Food Festival
Food lovers have a special treat in store for them with Al Qasba Food Festival.
Year on year this celebration grows bigger and better to include not only daily cooking shows and competitions, but also various entertainment activities. Al Qasba's walkways become alive with fun and entertainment, including musical shows and street performances, for the whole family. Each day of the festival features a different celebrity chef giving a full 180 minute demonstration. The festival also includes an exhibition of gourmet foods from commercial exhibitors and local talents and little chefs also have the chance to pick up some tricks at the Young Chef's Academy.

Coinciding with the event, Al Qasba organises lectures about the tenets of Quranic Healing and the importance of the foods that are mentioned in the Holy Quran. This is in addition to the 'UAE Green Festival' exhibition, a countrywide celebration designed specifically to educate people across the UAE about all the aspects of a green life.

Sharjah Children Reading festival

The Sharjah Children's Reading Festival (SCRF) takes place in April at the Sharjah Expo Centre. Arab and foreign publishing houses take part in the event with over 20,000 printed, audio-visual and electronic titles. SCRF hosts a number of guests including authors, intellectuals, artists and researchers in the field of children's literature, who participate in the parallel seminars, workshops and exhibitions, which is held as part of the official SCRF program.

SCRF also includes a series of art and heritage workshops, as well as theatrical plays, reading sessions, a play zone, circus performances, clown shows, special needs workshops, safety workshops, nutrition workshops and many other activities performed by guests from the GCC region, Arab world and Europe. In addition, the cookery corner which hosts famous chefs specializing in children's cuisine, SCRF awards children with books.

Sharjah Calligraphy Biennial

Sharjah Calligraphy Biennial has always been known to be of one of the most remarkable events taking place in the region. It aim at revealing the power of the letter in bringing cultures together. It is an art that reflects the spirit of the place and the existence.

The event is a celebration of Arabic calligraphy and its creators, and aims to make the world realise the beauty and authenticity of the Arabic letter. It introduces the features of Islamic civilization as it is a major form of artistic expression in Islamic cultures, especially and particularly in religious contexts.

Sharjah Biennial
Sharjah Biennial is organised by Sharjah Art Foundation, which brings a broad range of contemporary art and cultural programmes to the communities of Sharjah, the UAE and the region. Since 1993, Sharjah Biennial has commissioned, produced and presented large-scale public installations, performances, and films, offering artists from the region and beyond an internationally recognised platform for exhibition and experimentation.

Ramadan & Summer Shopping
In summer, the city of Sharjah offers ten weeks of fun and great entertainment for all. This annual event starts in the month of June running parallel to the sister emirate's Dubai Shopping Festival. Sharjah summer festival offers a large number of summer promotional activities, attractive discounts, deals, raffles and grand entertainment shows. Usually, these activities are organized to encourage people to shop during summer.

Sharjah Spring Festival takes place in the month of January. 1700 outlets selling a variety of different products make it one of region's biggest spring shows. The promotions offered at the festival include special discounts, fun and entertaining events and activities aimed at highlighting the tourism scene of Sharjah.

Sharjah International Book Fair
Sharjah International Book Fair is a ten-day marathon event held every year in November. Last year the event attracted 400,000 visitors from nearly 42 countries, along with hundreds of publishers from all over the world.

National Day
Every year, on December 2nd the entire emirate of Sharjah turns green, red, black and white to celebrate the independence of the UAE. Glittering fireworks, musical parades and traffic jams are all part of the UAE's National Day Celebrations.

Chinese Commodities Fair Sharjah
Chinese Commodities Fair Sharjah (CCFS) has emerged as the largest in the Middle East for Chinese goods, and one of the most prominent platforms promoting Chinese products in the Middle East.

The CCFS is considered to be a major booster in the trade relations between China and the GCC states as a whole and the UAE in particular.

Aiming to bridge the gap between the Arab World and China, CCFS is once again set to help businesses from both sides to explore better opportunities and strengthen existing ties and cooperation.

Beaches & Parks
Parks

The Municipality maintains Sharjah beautifully landscaped parks of which there are over 40 spread around the city.

Admission is usually free of charge with the exception of Al Muntaza and Sharjah Desert Park. Opening hours vary from park to park but the weekends are the busiest. Whether large or small, all the parks have green lawns; purpose built play and seating areas and a variety of sports pitches (usually basketball, volleyball and football). All parks have a list of do's and don'ts at the entrance advising if football, barbecues or cycling is allowed. Many parks let you take in food and drink, so you can have a picnic in the peaceful, green setting. The smoking of Sheesha pipes is not permitted in public.

Opening hours may change during the Holy Month of Ramadan and during summer, with parks opening and closing later in the day.

The city beaches on the Arabian Gulf coast offer safe, white, sandy palm lined beaches with clear blue seas and gently shelving shores. The public beaches below offer free access, but have limited facilities. The most popular beaches for sunbathing are Al Khan Beach and Al Mamzar. The Corniche Beach is packed over the weekends and is not really suitable for sunbathers. The east coast has beautiful bays lined with sandy beaches and crystal clear waters. Famous for its water sports, snorkeling, diving and relaxing, this coast creates the ideal break for a weekend, either camping on the beach or staying in the motels and hotels that line the coast.

The sun can be strong, so hats, sun cream and UV protection suits are a must at any time of the year. Dress restrictions do apply on the Sharjah beaches and ladies should be suitably attired.

Al Montazah Park
Spread over a wide expanse, Al Montazah is touted as Sharjah's first-ever family entertainment destination, with the first of its kind water park among a host of other amusement and recreational attractions. Envisioned to be the epitome of 'happiness' for families, the park lies on an island right in the heart of the emirate, stretching against the scenic backdrop of Sharjah's picturesque skyline. Despite fun being our first priority, Al Montazah boasts as well the best international safety standards from high aesthetic values and world-class infrastructure. Care for the environment and the varying needs for leisure in a relaxed ambience are the hallmarks of Sharjah's new destination for family recreation.

Sharjah National Park
This is Sharjah's biggest park covering 630,000 square metres and is located at Intersection No. 5, Sharjah/Al Dhaid Road. This park opens weekday afternoons from 2 - 6 pm and all day at the weekends, and 10 am – 7pm on public holidays.

Green Belt Park
Green Belt Park (for women only) lies in the northeast part of the city of Sharjah, close to Cultural Square. The park also features water fountains and an open theatre with four main gates.

Al Majaz Park
Al Majaz Park is one of the modern public gardens in the city and is close to the Khaled Lagoon. It has a central area for holding ceremonies and is a very popular place with plenty of child-friendly facilities.

Al Majaz Waterfront
Al Majaz Waterfront project brings together the history and culture of Sharjah to create a well-rounded family-leisure and entertainment experience. Featuring special attractions including a new kids area, landscaped gardens, cafes, shops, kiosks and the 100-meter height and 200 meters wide Sharjah fountain - one of the region's largest water features, the Al Majaz Waterfront is the premier leisure area of the city.

Al Khan Beach
Al Khan Beach stretches from the old village in Al Khan to Al Layyeh power station and it is one of the safest beaches in the UAE. This beach is very popular with the tourists, especially during weekends and holidays.

Al Corniche Beach
Palm trees surround the sandy beach, stretching out from Sharjah Ladies Club along the coast to Coral Beach Resort.

Khorfakkan Beaches
The private Oceanic Hotel beach is a great location to relax or enjoy water sports, for a fee. You can have a pleasant and delightful time

swimming or barbecuing along the coast where many rocky outcrops are found. There are also charming sandy beaches and areas allocated for camping in Khorfakkan.

Khaled Lagoon & Al Buheirah Corniche
The Khaled Lagoon is a large expanse of water with a beautiful fountain in its centre. The lagoon is surrounded by green lawns and palm trees plus walking paths of the Al Buheirah Corniche. This area is one of the most densely populated areas of Sharjah. Visitors enjoy walking around the lagoon, passing Al Jazeera Park and the Central Souk. A walking tour of the entire Khaled Lagoon takes about an hour and covers a distance of 6½ kilometers. There are a large number of restaurants and cafes in which to relax around the lagoon as well, particularly at the Al Majaz Waterfront - which includes the Sharjah fountain - one of the region's biggest water fountains, modern gardens, cafes, shops, kiosks, and a specially designed kids area.

Sharjah Corniche
The Sharjah Corniche stretches from Al Buheirah Corniche to Ajman Beach, passing by the fish market. It is a destination for walkers covering a considerable distance and following the creek, and then the coast.

Beaches
The city beaches on the Arabian Gulf coast offer safe, white, sandy palm lined stretches of sand with clear blue seas. Public beaches below offer free access but have limited facilities. The most popular

beaches for sunbathing are Al Khan Beach and Al Mamzar. The Corniche Beach is packed over the weekends and is not really suitable for sunbathers. Sharjah's east coast has beautiful bays lined with sandy beaches and crystal clear waters. Famous for water sports, snorkelling, diving and relaxing, this coast creates the ideal break for a weekend, either camping on the beach or staying in any of the motels and hotels that line the coast.

The sun can be strong, so hats, sun cream and UV protection suits are a must at any time of the year. Dress restrictions do apply on the Sharjah beaches and ladies should be suitably attired.

Sports & Activities

From the west coast to the east, there's so much to explore no matter whether you want to be active, adventurous or just kick back and relax.

It's not just the heritage that attracts visitors to Sharjah. It is the only emirate with territory on both coasts, so you can swim from a city beach, hike through the mountains, dive in the Indian Ocean and kayak through the world's most northerly mangrove forest, all without leaving Sharjah.

Sharjah is a great adventure sport destination, from offroading to diving; adrenaline junkies are well catered for. If you prefer ball sports to extreme sports, you won't be disappointed; from the UAE's original rugby club to one of its newest golf courses, Sharjah has it all, and, when the weather heats up, keep cool at the emirate's ice rinks and bowling alleys. Fancy yourself as a sure shot? Make the most of Sharjah's top class archery and shooting ranges.

Water sports fans are in for a treat. Kayak trips of KhorFakkan mangroves are exercise, nature and education all rolled into one. World championship powerboat races are exciting spectacles. And traditional Arabian sports, such as camel racing shouldn't be missed.

All this activity aside, those who view a holiday as a chance for relaxation will find a collection of spas and beauty salons where top treatments are surprisingly reasonably priced.

Golf
Sharjah Golf & Shooting Club
Boasting a fully floodlit, Peter Harradine designed 9 hole course, this is Sharjah's first fully grassed course. Played twice, the course is a par 72 in excess of 7,300 yards, and with between five and seven tee positions on each hole, it offers considerable variety and interest; and that's before you negotiated the water hazards and bunkers. The Academy's facilities include a 300m fully grassed driving range, 6,425 square metre world class short game area and 1,095 square metre putting green; all of which are fully floodlit. The club is welcoming to members and guests of all levels, with PGA professionals on hand to

offer expert tuition. Coaching programmes are suitable for all ages, and equipment is available for hire.

Shooting
Sharjah Golf & Shooting Club
Facilities include ranges for indoor pistols, rifles and revolvers and 25m and 50m German Technology ranges. Weapons range from specialised target pistols to .22 M16s. Safety is of paramount importance and a fully trained safety instructor accompanies visitors at all times.

Sharjah Ladies Club
Established under the patronage of Her Highness Sheikha Jawahar bint Mohammad Al Qassimi, the 14 lanes are open to both air pistol and air rifle shooters. The facility has enabled the creation of a women's national shooting team. Instruction is available. The club is a luxurious five-star setup on the coast near to the Radisson Blu resort and is a haven of pampering as well as shooting.

Archery
Sharjah Golf & Shooting Club
Target archery, using state of the art equipment, is offered at the indoor 20 yard range at SGSC. Tuition is available for all levels from qualified trainers and competitions are held throughout the year. The range is open Saturday to Thursday from 12:00 to 22:00 and from 14:00 to 22:00 on Fridays.

Horse Riding
Sharjah Equestrian & Racing Club

Established in 1982, SERC is one of the UAE's top equestrian facilities with one of the largest indoor riding facilities in the Middle East. The riding school is supervised by qualified international trainers and schooled horses are available for children and beginners. Pony tours are offered for young children at a cost. Group lessons are also available.

Ice Skating
Sharjah Ladies Club
To maintain your physical fitness, Sharjah Ladies Club offers its clients this unique facility for recreation, enjoyment, fun, and pleasure. From beginners to the most advanced, skaters can join a pleasant environment. Professional supervision and instruction is provided.

Sky 24
Taking sports, leisure and entertainment to a pretty high level, Sky 24 offers a great chance to get out of the heat on a sweltering summer's day.

Off-Roading
Most car rental agencies offer visitors 4WDs capable of desert driving. If renting a 4WD, make sure you get the details of the insurance plan, as many rental insurers won't cover damage caused by off-roading. Dune bashing, or desert driving, is one of the toughest challenges for both car and driver, but once you have mastered it, it's a lot of fun. If you do venture out into the desert, it is a good idea to have at least one experienced driver and one other car to help tow you out if you

get stuck. Most major tour companies offer a range of desert and mountain safaris if you'd rather leave the driving to the professionals. Driving in wadis is usually a bit more straightforward. Wadis are (usually) dry gullies, carved through the rock by rushing floodwaters, following the course of seasonal rivers. The main safety precautions to take when wadi bashing is to keep your eyes open for rare, but not impossible, thunderstorms developing. The wadis can fill up quickly and you will need to make your way to higher ground pretty fast to avoid flash floods.

Watersports & Diving
Sharjah is unique among the emirates in having coast on both the Arabian Gulf and the Gulf of Oman, making it a dream destination for watersports lovers. The calm waters, sheltered coves and pristine beaches are ideal for getting out on the water and many of the beach hotels offer the opportunity to both guests and non-guests, although the latter may have to pay a beach fee. Many have equipment for sea kayaking, sailing and windsurfing and some may offer waterskiing.

Fishing
The fishing is good, particularly off the east coast, and many people come in search of big game fish as well as eating fish. The sport is superb, often fierce and frenetic, but at the end of it there is always a willing restaurant chef happy to barbeque your catch.

Kayaking

Kayaking is a wonderful way to get up close to nature and explore the coast and inshore waters. Weaving your way pas the gnarled trunks and overhanging branches of the mangrove forest, you may encounter turtles, crabs, and even the critically endangered (there are only around 50 breeding pairs) Halcyon Chloris Kalbaensis, or white-collared kingfisher which is unique to this small area.

Diving
Diving is popular and the clear waters off the east coast are home to a variety of marine species, coral life and even shipwrecks. You'll see exotic fish, possibly moray eels, small sharks, barracuda, stingrays, sea snakes and even turtles. Another option for diving enthusiasts is a trip to Musanadam. Part of the Sultanate of Oman, it is often described as the 'Norway of the Middle East' due to it's many inlets and cliffs that plunge straight into the sea. Sheer wall dives with strong currents and clear waters are more suitable for advanced divers, while huge bays with their calm waters and bountiful shallow reefs are ideal for the less experienced. Courses are offered under the usual international training organisations.

Camel Racing
This is a chance to see a truly traditional local sport, though now with a modern twist as the camels are steered by 'robot' jockeys, controlled by an operator in one of the gleaming 4WDs that follow the races. Races take place in the winter months and additional meetings are often held on public holidays. Races are usually held early on Thursday

or Friday mornings, but you should see camels out being exercised during the day in the cooler months. Sharjah's camel racecourse is near Al Dhaid, and there are tracks in each of the other emirates too.

Horse Racing & Showjumping
Sharjah Equestrian & Racing Club
Horseracing in the UAE is great sport and big business, running from November all the way through to the world's richest horserace, the Dubai World Cup, in late March. Sharjah Spectator Sports holds meetings through the season, on Saturday afternoons with six or seven races per meeting at 30 minute intervals with the first race at about 14:00. Entrance is free to all racecourses in the UAE and soft drinks and light snacks are available. A Pick Six competition to select the winners of each race is held at every meeting with big prizes on offer. Results of the competition are announced in the paddock following the final race. There are regular showjumping and dressage competitions throughout the season, from November to March. There are also a whole series of events for purebred Arabians. In Sharjah all events are held at the equestrian and racing club, but there are also events across the UAE.

Paintballing
Sharjah Golf & Shooting Club
The Paintball Park at SGSC is world famous and is amongst the very best in the Middle East. The extraordinary and exciting floodlit park can accommodate up to 150 players in one session in teams of up to

14 players. There are two phases, the 5,000 square metre jungle phase (complete with bunkers, trees, hills, trenches, bridges, hut and even an old aircraft), and the Sahara phase; you can also indulge in a spot of target practise to help hone your skills. The park is run by friendly and qualified marshals and state of the art equipment is provided and for sale in the pro shop. The park is open from 10:00 to 22:00 and refreshments and changing rooms are available.

Bowling
Bowling is a great indoor activity for the long hot days of summer. It is available at Ewan Bowling Centre at Ewan Hotel, Radisson Blu and Sky 24 at Al Durrah Tower.

Cricket
Second only to football in popularity, impromptu cricket matches can be found on most areas of wasteland on Fridays and during the evenings. Sharjah is also home to the 27,000 capacity Sharjah Cricket Association Stadium which, between 1984 and 2003, hosted One Day International tournaments involving the world's top teams. The stadium has been designated as the home ground for Afghanistan's national cricket team for all One Day Internationals and first class matches; they also have full use of the facilities at Al Dhaid cricket village. Al Dhaid cricket village is a 10,000 capacity venue used by international teams for training and as the host of local competitions including the Al Dhaid Ramadan Cup. Sharjah Cricket Stadium also played host to the Bangladesh Twenty20 League in 2010.

Dhow Cruises
There are many operators who offer cruises sailing north from Dibba following the coastline where steep rocky cliffs rise out of the sea. You'll pass small fishing villages and will hopefully see dolphins and turtles, and have the chance to snorkel in the pristine waters. Prices start at around Dhs.200 per adult for a full day, including lunch, refreshments and snorkelling gear. Cruises depart from the Omani side of Dibba and can be arranged by most hotels or tour operators. Dhow cruises also operate around Khalid Lagoon and offer a great opportunity to view the modern city from the form of transport that first defined it and brought it fame and wealth.

Traditional dhow races, rowing races and even dragon boat races are often organised in the waters of one of the city's lagoons, offshore from the Corniche or in the bay at KhorFakkan over on the east coast.

Power boating
On the west coast, Sharjah's Khalid Lagoon plays host to the Sharjah Formula 1 Powerboat Grand Prix as part of the annual Water Festival, held in December. Described as being akin to driving a Formula 1 car across a ploughed field, it is one of the most spectacular and exciting sports in the world, and, as the season finale, Sharjah is its most dramatic home. The boats reach speeds of up to 225kph (130mph) as they race around the buoyed course.

Football

The 'beautiful game' is as popular in Sharjah as it is across the rest of the planet. If you're in need of an organized game while you're in Sharjah, head for Sharjah Wanderers. Impromptu games happen throughout the emirate although it is at Kalba on the east coast that you cannot move for friendly matches; visitors are often welcomed as extra players

Desert & Adventures

The ever-shifting sands found inland from all the major coastal settlements create an endless variety of landscapes, colours and vegetation. The beautiful desert of Sharjah attracts visitors, who are impressed by the vastness and charm of the desert. There is nothing compared to watching a sunset in the serene dunes of Sharjah's desert.

Dune bashing
Desert driving is an art in its own right. There is plenty of sand to practice on within 15 minutes of the city, but please keep to the tracks. Tour operators will arrange desert safaris including sand skiing and even courses in sand driving. 4-wheel drive vehicles can be hired from most rental companies but make sure you have some experience before venturing into the unknown, and always go with at least one other vehicle.

Perhaps the closest you will get to experience the real Arabia is to take a drive out of the city and into the sands. The impressive hilly outcrop of Fossil Rock is surrounded by rolling red sand dunes and lies not far from Al Dhaid. This is a popular area for dune driving, quad biking (available for hire), fossil hunting and camping.

Quad biking

These noisy but 'fun on four' wheel bikes can be hired in the vicinity of Fossil Rock (S116 Meliha Road going toward Kalba – turn right at the Mahafeez roundabout with the mast, turn left after about 5 kilometres and continue along this road until you see the quad bike area on your left). The area is fenced off with sections to suit various ages. Helmets are provided.

Wadi Trips

The impressive Al Hajar Mountain range offers spectacular drives amid high, rugged scenery. Criss-cross the mountains between Manama, Masafi and the east coast, visit the famous Hatta Pools with their deep canyons, or go further south where green and water filled wadis can be found near Al Ain.

Wadi: The Arabic name for a valley, usually with a dry river bed. In times of heavy rainfall, a wadi is not the place to be as floods do occur. Water builds up in the mountains and is released in a wall of water, which gushes down the valley taking boulders, palm trees and even vehicles with it.

Culture & Heritage

From the days of the early trading with the East to the settlement of the Qawasim seafaring tribe, Sharjah was the most important port on the lower Arabian Gulf.

The fascinating past of the UAE has ensured that present and future generations have a great historical and cultural heritage to be proud of. The glorious monuments and heritage sites in the region stand quietly today to retell their story of the past.

The older generations recall that their expertise with desert life was crucial to their own survival. These skills are still held in high esteem by many of the local inhabitants. Today's visitors can experience desert life through participating in a range of organized trips and by enjoying a memorable night spent under the stars.

Other aspects of the UAE's culture can be found by visiting places such as the fishing harbours or fish souks, boat-building yards, falconry centres, gold and spice souks and other venues. There are also various events that are organized in the UAE to encourage interest and appreciation of the heritage and culture of the region. These events range from exhibitions, theatrical shows, sporting activities, dhow and camel races, and a host of other cultural activities.

Sharjah has been transformed under the vision and guidance of His Highness Sheikh Dr. Sultan Bin Mohammed Al Qasimi into a vibrant and bustling metropolis while preserving the core values of tradition, heritage and culture.

In a region where history is often measured in terms of decades, every cultural aspect is precious. Preserving the heritage of the past remains essential to cultivating a national identity. Sharjah's rich and varied cultural and commercial achievements are based on solid foundations and traditional heritage. More than 20 museums and heritage sites provide the perfect platform to showcase the arts, crafts, traditions and importance of Islam in the lifestyle of the people in this most fascinating city.

To enable Sharjah to continue to be at the forefront of cultural development and heritage preservation in the region, His Highness Sheikh Dr. Sultan Bin Mohammed Al Qasimi issued a decree to establish the Department of Culture and Information. The role of the department is to initiate and organize cultural activities across the emirate and to create a platform for interaction between Islam and other cultures.

Sharjah's old city was restored just a decade ago, transforming the former homes of prominent families into museums showcasing the region's heritage. Culture illuminates every facet of the emirate, providing context to all generations, a rhythm to the everyday. From classical to contemporary the cultural appeal is immediate and exciting.

There are ancient archaeological sites and cutting-edge contemporary art exhibitions, great houses of learning and the opportunity to join energetic traditional pastimes. Historic culture is championed in unrivalled educational centres, an extraordinary array of world-class museums, and the lovingly restored Heritage Area. Authentic Arabian culture can be seen at the scholarly Dr. Sultan Al Qasimi Centre of Gulf Studies or for shopping enthusiasts at the renovated souks and attractions highlight everything from trade to transport.

Classical culture is celebrated in the very architecture of the emirate. Islamic culture is at Sharjah's heart, great buildings house the leading educational institutions of Sharjah's University City, and theatre, music and visual arts are championed in both traditional and modern forms. Contemporary cultural life in Sharjah is busy and attractive, from the cafes of Al Qasba to inspiring art galleries and exciting festivals. The landscape itself encourages traditional pastimes and leisure pursuits. For all ages, from all cultures, Sharjah's cultural enthusiasm is infectious.

Sharjah Arts Area
Located adjacent to the picturesque corniche is the Sharjah Arts Area. This area comprises of a handful of exquisitely restored traditional houses, as well as an 18th century mosque. This truly unique area is home to not only the Sharjah Arts Museum but also the Sharjah Arts

Centre, the Sharjah Art Gallery, the Emirates Fine Arts Society and the Very Special Art Centre.

Located in the area is Bait Al Serkal, which was initially the home of the British Comissioner for the coast of Oman and later home to Sharjah's first hospital. There are a lot of facilities available in Bait Al Serkal such as the Art Cafe, which serves delicious local cuisine.

In the surrounding area, artisan galleries are housed in Obaid Al Shamsi's house and the yard has been converted into a place for the disabled, to provide an arena for those with special needs to practice and exhibit their art.

Sharjah Art Museum, which was opened in 1997, is the Gulf's biggest art museum. It consists of thirty-two exhibition halls, eight of which house unique private collections generously donated by His Highness Sheikh Dr. Sultan Bin Mohammed Al Qasimi. The Sharjah Art Museum offers exciting exhibition programs which encompass both classical and modern art from local and international artists.

Heart of Sharjah Area
Heart of Sharjah Area is a testament of Sharjah's dedication to preserving the cultural history of its predecessors. It is celebrated as the foundation of the accolade from UNESCO, which established Sharjah as the Cultural Capital of the Arab World.

In Heart of Sharjah Area, you will see handcrafted works of art and objects that date back to a time when local people relied solely on fishing and pearling. Trace the development of education, currency and the early postal system. Discover the traditional skills and crafts relating to jewellery, costumes, herbal medicine, music and folklore.

Sharjah Art Foundation
Located in Sharjah's historic Art and Heritage Areas, Sharjah Art Foundation activities and events take place throughout the year and include exhibitions featuring the work of Arab and international artists, performances, music, film screenings and artist talks as well as extensive art education programmes for children, adults and families. The Foundation hosts the annual March Meeting and every two years presents the Sharjah Biennial.

Museums
Preserved in time, this is Sharjah before the discovery of oil when it was the most important port in the region and wealthy on trade, seafaring and pearls.

Take a tour through the Heart of Sharjah Area and be inspired by the architecture and simplicity of a lifestyle that thrived long ago. Discover a world of knowledge with over twenty state-of-the-art museums and explore the history of Sharjah which dates back more than 6000 years.

Sharjah Maritime Museum

The Sharjah Maritime Museum was first opened in the Heritage Area in early 2003 to highlight the maritime life of the UAE. However, due to the importance of the sea and its significance in the region's heritage, the museum was expanded and relocated in Al Khan in 2009. The sea has played a key role in Sharjah's development and was the primary reason for the first settlers choosing this site over 6,000 years ago.

In the museum you can explore traditional wooden seafaring dhows used for fishing, trading and pearling, each designed according to their use. See genuine Arabian pearls, discover how they were collected, measured and weighed. Admire the powerful wooden pulley blocks used to raise and lower sails and discover the local traditions for catching fish.

Sharjah Calligraphy Museum
The Sharjah Calligraphy Museum was opened in 2002 in the building of the house of Hamad Al Midfaa in the Sharjah Heritage Area (Heart of Sharjah). Enter this museum and you embark on a fascinating journey of discovery across centuries of Arabian heritage in the form of beautifully written script.

Created by local artists and well-known international calligraphers, significant works of art from the Arab world demonstrate the complexity of this vibrant art form and its historical and Islamic foundations. Arabic calligraphy seen on canvas, wood, paper and ceramics will inspire you with its positive and living energy.

Al Eslah School Museum

Established in 1935 as the first formal educational institute to be opened in Sharjah, this school welcomed pupils from all over the Gulf region.

Experience school life as it was some 70 years ago while sitting at the wooden desks in the shaded classrooms and imagine attending an Islamic school. See images of the people that brought education to life and visit the Headmaster's Room to admire the Holy Quran stands made from palm wood. During term time, students from overseas would spend their nights in the upstairs dormitory.

Sharjah Art Museum

Walk into a world of artistic excellence and expression. Opened in April 1997 this is the largest art museum in the Gulf with both temporary exhibitions and permanent collections by renowned artists. Explore the history of the region through the Orientalist painters of the 18th and 19th centuries, as well as gallery after gallery of stunning landscapes, cityscapes and portraits painted in oil, water colours and acrylics, created by both local and internationally renowned artists.

Sharjah Museum of Islamic Civilization

The Sharjah Museum of Islamic Civilization was renovated and re-opened in 2008 as a significant tourist landmark in the region, and the first of its kind in the UAE. Situated right at the historical heart of Sharjah on the Majarrah Waterfront, this fascinating Museum started its life as a traditional Middle Eastern souq or indoor market.

The museum's predecessor was called the Islamic Museum, and was situated in one of the heritage houses in the Heritage Area. It was established in 1996, and continued to receive visitors until 2007, before transferring to its new location as the Sharjah Museum of Islamic Civilization.

The building now transformed into a state-of-the art cultural venue, the new Sharjah Museum of Islamic Cvilization, houses more than five thousand exquisite Islamic artefacts from all over the Islamic World, arranged according to themes over seven spacious galleries and display areas.

Al Mahatta Museum
In 1932 the first airport in the United Arab Emirates opened in Sharjah, used as a staging post for commercial flights en route from Britain to India.

From man's first attempts to fly to landing on the moon, explore the history of flight and the development of aviation in this region at the museum which is located in Sharjah's first airport building. Watch an interesting film about the daily life at the airport and Sharjah Town during the 1930's and experience first hand this fascinating period of

Sharjah's history. Four of the original propeller planes, fully restored, stand guard in the hangar alongside the original refueling tanker.

Sharjah Science Museum
The Sharjah Science Museum, which first opened in 1996, now has more than 50 interactive displays suitable for all ages.

Bringing science to life, this museum has so many exhibits and interactive displays designed to stimulate and inspire the visitor.

Whatever your age, have fun discovering science with hands-on experiments and illusions, exploring colour, aerodynamics, cryogenics and physiology. Take part in Electricity demonstration, probe the secrets of space and test your reactions and strength. Even toddlers can discover their curiosity about the world around us, in their very own play area.

Sharjah Archaeology Museum
The Sharjah Archaeology Museum first opened in 1993. It was moved to its current location in 1997 and serves as a permanent archive for all archaeological findings recovered in the Emirate of Sharjah since the start of archaeological excavations in 1972.

Uncover the stories of Sharjah's very early history, brought alive in this interesting museum.

Explore the changing environments experienced by the region's inhabitants from the Stone Age to the present day through displays of artefacts, coins, jewellery, pottery and ancient weapons. Investigate a dig in progress, explore models of burials, houses and tombs and see the first forms of writing in this area.

Sharjah Aquarium
The Sharjah Aquarium opened in Al Khan Old area in 2008. Covering an area of 6500m², and consisting of two floors equipped with 20 water aquariums, each of which is filled with 1.8 million liters of water, it is the largest government learning center in the UAE.

Submerge yourself in the colourful, rich and diverse undersea world that is home to a variety of marine life native to the seas around us.

With over 250 species there is so much to see from the smallest clown fish and delicate seahorses to moray eels, rays and reef sharks. Take a journey underwater and discover everything from the larger ocean creatures to the smaller marine life to be found in the rock pools, coral reefs, lagoons and mangroves.

Sharjah Discovery Center
This children's centre is a great day's outing for the whole family with seven themed areas, packed full of 'hands on activities' and plenty of fun.

Filled with action and entertainment, enter a colourful arena exploring the dynamics of water, the five senses, the art of travel and the mechanisms of building, become a star on TV, climb the wall and 'shop till you drop' in the children's supermarket.

Sharjah Heritage Museum

The Sharjah Heritage Museum was re-opened in the Heritage Area (Heart of Sharjah) in 2012 as part of an expansion plan, the original museum first opened in early 2003. The museum is dedicated to highlighting Sharjah's rich traditions, customs and culture as a source of pride and inspiration to the people of the UAE and its visitors.

Discover the 'Landscape', 'Lifestyle', 'Celebrations', 'Livelihood', 'Traditional Knowledge' and 'Oral Traditions' of Sharjah's rich heritage as you take on a journey through the museum's six galleries.

Majlis Al Midfa

The most peaceful meeting place is renowned for its remarkable round windtower, the only one of its kind in the UAE. Step back in time and enter a world where the men of the family and their male guests would gather to discuss affairs of the day. Amongst the many interesting items donated by the family, you will see a carved pearl chest, old books and manuscripts and a silver dagger with gold leave decoration.

The museum commemorates the late Ibrahim bin Mohammed al Midfa, a prominent intellectual figure who contributed ommensely to the cultural development in the UAE in general, and Sharjah in particular. In 1927 Al Midfa issued the first newspaper in the history of the UAE – the Oman newspaper; he subsequently issued Soutul Asafeer (the Sound of Birds).

Bait Sheikh Saeed Bin Hamed Al Qasimi – Kalba
No trip to Sharjah is complete without exploring the Emirate's East Coast. Sandy beaches, scenic mountains, lush mangroves and heritage sites await you. In Kalba, you will find a charismatic old fort and the prominent beachside residence of H.E. Sheikh Saeed bin Hamad Al Qasimi, both fully restored to display items of Islamic heritage and lifestyle, archaeological finds, weapons, agricultural equipment, in addition to a collection of musical instruments. Inland, in a beautiful setting overlooking the mangroves is Al Ghail Fort.

Owned by Sheikh Saeed Bin Hamad Al Qasimi, the house was built between 1898 and 1901, and was designed to preserve the artistic and traditional identity of the Gulf architecture and Islamic pan-Arabian style.

Built in a rectangular shape, the house is divided into two sections, eastern and western. The eastern section includes the Access, the Majlis, Morabba'a, the defensive barrage with its shooting outlets (Mazaghil) and the inner Majlis facing the shore. This section, which is separated from the other by a wall in the middle, is designated for receiving men and guests while the western section comprises the living units and serving facilities allotted for women, children and servants.

Sharjah Fort (Al Hisn)
An Eye Opener to Sharjah's Glory

Step back in time to experience the most important building in Sharjah since the early nineteenth century to the mid-twentieth century. Built in 1823, the historic fort still stands majestically in the Heart of Sharjah resembling the days it was used as the seat of Sharjah's Government, the residence of the Al Qasimi ruling family, and a jail.

On your journey through the museum you will encounter a variety of fascinating galleries that offer a wide range of photographs, objects, stories that provide visitors with a unique opportunity to experience the history that has shaped Sharjah and its people.

See how daily life was experienced within the fort and observe the astounding changes Sharjah has experienced over the last two centuries. Find out what prison life was like inside Al Muhalwasa jail, learn how to make dibs (date molasses) and have a stimulating conversation inside the traditional majlis (sitting room). You can also examine weapons similar to those once used to protect Al Hisn and discover defense strategies used by the sheikhs and their guards.

Bait Al Naboodah
Bait Al Naboodah opened its doors as a museum in 1995. The house originally belonged to the late Obaid bin Eissa Bin Ali Al Shamsi, nicknamed Al Naboodah, who was a prominent pearl trader that held commercial ties with India, Africa and France. Al Naboodah lived in this house, which was built in 1845, with his wife and seven children.

Here at this charming two-storey house from 1845, you can admire traditional Gulf architecture in an age before air conditioning. Built around a large courtyard you can see walls made from coral, admire innovative methods of 'air conditioning' and unique decorative carvings, in both plaster and wood. Learn about daily family life and routines through displayed work by Arabian craftsmen in a bygone era.

Landmarks

Sharjah, land of diversified architectural character, has a landmark in every corner that narrates the story of the emirate's rich heritage and culture.

Starting from traditional souks like Souk Al Arsa, to state-of-the-art souks and malls like the Central Souk, and ending with Al Qasba and Al Majaz Waterfront which offer high-class and modern entertainment, cultural and leisure facilities, Sharjah is a warm and welcoming emirate.

Sharjah Islamic Culture Capital Monument 2014

The Sharjah Islamic Culture Capital memorial rises 42 meters and the podium occupies an area of 650 square meters, while the total area of the base that carries the highest column monument is 50 square meters. The bottom diameter of the column is 3.3 meters, while the upper diameter is 6.2 meters. The podium is covered with three different types of granite while the base column is covered with fibre glass, concrete and granite. The main column is covered with green granite, and surrounded by a spiral bar made of aluminum with different finishes creating a kind of contrast for easy reading of the verses of Holy Qur'an. The 28 Quranic verses celebrate reverence and quest for knowledge, learning and the merit of scholars. The upper part of the memorial includes 12 columns which are connected with 12 arches topped by a golden dome.

Al Majaz Amphitheatre
Dubbed the official venue of the Sharjah Capital of Islamic Culture (SICC) 2014 Celebrations, Al Majaz open-air Roman-style amphitheater is the first in the region.

The semi-circular theater includes several terraced seating areas that can accommodate up to 4500 spectators, and a huge stage equipped with a state-of-the-art audio system. Positioned on Al Majaz Island, Khalid Lagoon with an area of 7238 square meters, the Amphitheatre is tucked between Flag Island in the north and Al Majaz Waterfront in the south, and finds itself just opposite Sharjah Hilton Hotel.

Al Noor Mosque
Inaugurated in 2005, Al Noor Mosque was built at orders from Her Highness Sheikha Jawaher Bint Mohammed Al Qasimi, spouse of His Highness Sheikh Dr. Sultan Bin Mohammed Al Qasimi, Supreme Council Member and Ruler of Sharjah.

With its elegance and creative design, this iconic masterpiece reflects the Ottoman architectural style with its minarets and huge domes.

Al Noor Mosque is the first mosque in Sharjah to open its doors to the expatriate community and visitors to Sharjah so that they may learn about the UAE National culture and religion.

Public visit every Monday at 10am (except public holidays)
Duration of the tour approx. 1 hour
Explanations on Islam & Culture of U.A.E
Questions and Answer session

Eye of The Emirates
Stands out as one of the most prominent landmarks in Sharjah. This giant ferris wheel is 60 meters high, which gives visitors a chance to view Sharjah, as well as parts of Dubai, from its 42 air-conditioned cabins which allow a view of up to 30 miles around.

King Faisal Mosque
King Faisal Mosque earns the honour of being the largest among Sharjah's mosques and named after King Faisal bin Abdul Aziz Al Saud, former Ruler of the Kingdom of Saudi Arabia. The mosque was opened in 1987 and can accommodate 16670 worshipers.

Note: Non-Muslims are not allowed for inside visit to this mosque

The Flag Island
Located in the city of Sharjah opposite the corniche area. The flagpole on Flag Island is the 7th tallest flagpole in the world, where the UAE

flag is flying on a 123 metre-high pole, and holds a flag of 15 x 30 meters.

The Flag Island was inaugurated by His Highness Sheikh Dr. Sultan bin Mohammed Al Qasimi, Member of the Supreme Council and Ruler of Sharjah, on December 2, 2012 as part of the UAE's 41st National Day celebration.

Al Rolla Square
The Rolla Square is a historical site in Sharjah and was named as such after the planting of the first banyan tree (locally known as Rolla tree) in the 1800s.

The tree lasted for nearly 150 years until 1978, and families from Dubai, Ajman and other emirates would gather near the Rolla tree and use it as a meeting point for Eid, National Day, meetings and other special occasions.

Cultural Capital of the Arab World Monument
In 1998, Sharjah was named the 'Cultural Capital of the Arab World' by UNESCO, an honour richly deserved. Sharjah has kept the spirit of its history alive by innovatively incorporating tradition into every aspect of contemporary development. The result is a vibrant, modern Emirate that simultaneously looks forward to a bright future as it looks back respectfully to its history.

Kuwait Square

This beautiful landmark was built to celebrate the strong relationship between the United Arab Emirate and Kuwait, and to serve as a permanent memorial to the brotherly bonds between the two nations that are joined together by the ties of kinship, unity of faith and language and take pride in a shared past and present and bright future.

His Highness Dr. Sheikh Sultan bin Mohammed Al Qasimi, Supreme Council Member and Ruler of Sharjah, had been the moving spirit behind the landmark project since its beginning and until its completion. The Kuwait Square was unveiled by the Ruler on Sunday, 25th February, 1990.

The memorial came up at the important intersection named after Kuwait and is at the heart of some of the busiest roads connecting with the city centre.

Al Ittihad Square
It is one of Sharjah's biggest square, covering an area of more than 60,000 square-meters in Al-Sour district. The union monument is placed in the middle of the area and is decorated with seven oysters each with a pearl inside which represent each of the seven Emirates. The seven oysters surround the central pillar, which is crowned with a golden pearl symbolizing the union of the Emirates.

Cultural Square

Sharjah's Cultural Square is one of the most impressive sights in the emirate of Sharjah, bounded on all sides by rich Islamic architecture and dominated by an awe-inspiring sculpture of the Holy Quran. The Square is home to the Ahmed Bin Hanbal Mosque, the Cultural Centre and the Diwan Al Amiree.

Central Souk
Think of 'shopping in Sharjah' and the Central Souk springs to mind. Open since 1979, the legendary Central Souk is the most famous souk in Sharjah and is a must-see destination for all shoppers. Discover an extraordinary collection of handicrafts, brilliant in colour and magnetic in appeal.

Delve into a maze of more than 600 exciting and intriguing shops split between two levels with spacious corridors that take you from store to store, to uncover unusual treasures and traditional gift items, handmade goods and regional imports. You will find a mixture of shops selling gold, silver, authentic jewellery, precious stones, beautiful modern jewellery, to impressive collections of Oriental carpets and rugs, arts, crafts and attractive ornaments, cameras, models of traditional Arab dhows (sailing vessels) in silver; Indian, Pakistani, Indonesian and African hand-carved furniture and products, precious Arabic perfumes and cosmetics, textiles, beaded bags, exquisite Afghani embroideries, shawls in brilliant colours, embroidered Syrian table cloths, antiques and copper trays in all sizes, and much more.

The Central Souk has one of the best selections of oriental carpets in the UAE. Many outlets specialise in carpets, kilims, elegant silk carpets, carpetbags and wall hangings, which come from Afghanistan, Turkey, Iran, Kashmir, Pakistan and anywhere between Central Asia and China. Most of the carpet sellers are knowledgeable about their trade and they will order you a traditional cup of tea or coffee and happily unroll carpet after carpet until you find the one you want.

In between shopping and discovering, relax and enjoy a snack in the friendly cafés followed by a wander along the scenic Khaled Lagoon.

Souk Al Arsah
Step back in time and visit the peaceful air-conditioned alleyways of the covered market, probably the oldest market place in the UAE, designed with solid wooden doors, beautiful coral brick walls and hanging lanterns. The shopkeepers are friendly, helpful and more than happy to relate stories about their particular craft or business whilst sharing a glass of suleimani (spicy tea with a delicious sweet flavour) or a mint tea. The souk features a number of small stores selling local, new and antique handicrafts, wooden Arabic bridal and pearl chests, copper coffee pots, ethnic and hand-made jewellery, perfume bottles and incense, handmade woven garments, palm-leaf baskets, medicinal herbs, carpets, shawls and novelties.

Al Qasba

Al Qasba is a unique waterfront destination centrally located in Sharjah city. With the Etisalat Eye of the Emirates observation wheel in the background, the lively banks of Al Qasba offer a range of trendy restaurants and cafés serving cuisines from around the world.

Welcoming families, business visitors and tourists alike, Al Qasba combines culture with entertainment and continuously strives to develop leisure activities that highlight Arabic and Islamic heritage.

Al Majaz waterfront

Featuring special attractions including landscaped gardens, cafes, shops, kiosks andthe 100-meter height and 200 meters wide Sharjah fountain, Al Majaz waterfront is an ideal venue for a relaxed breakfast, healthy lunch, dinner with the family, late night coffee, or a business meeting any time of day. The picture-perfect backdrop of the musical cybernetic Sharjah Fountain, a key feature of the project, makes dining at the Al Majaz Waterfront restaurants and cafes a sheer delight.

Al Noor Island

Sharjah's newest leisure attraction has been designed and developed to inspire the senses with spacious landscaped areas, innovative architecture and multi-media experiences.

The 45,470 square meter Island located in Khalid Lagoon in Sharjah was provided with atmospheric lighting, the subtle lighting of island features with LEDs and other light installations, bring the island to life at night. A number of art installations from around the world provide further inspiration for visitors, including the 'OVO', 'Torus' and various light paintings visible after dark.

Al Noor Island's new Butterfly House is expected to provide a big draw for residents and visitors to Sharjah. With ornamentally perforated shadow roof inspired by ornate Arab windows (mashrabiya), the aviary will house as many as 500 exotic butterflies native to a variety of countries. Butterfly species include the African Monarch (*Danaus chrysippus*), the Autumn Leaf (*Doleschallia bisaltide*) from India and the Common Rose swallow-tail butterfly (*Pachliopta aristolochiae*), which is found across South East Asia and is known for its bright colouration and unique pattern of its wings.

The Butterfly House will also have a gift shop and a modern café for visitors, with indoor and outdoor seating area. Nearby, visitors will find a Literature Pavilion, where they can relax, read, take in the beauty of nature around them. The island features a 3,500 meter long walkway which takes visitors through the miniature gardens to key facilities, whilst allowing them to take in the peaceful setting and view outdoor art attractions.

Nature & Reserves

From beaches, marshes and mangroves to acacia forests and date palm groves, the narrow coast of the UAE on the Indian Ocean offers many different habitats.

Biologically diverse, Kalba's sanctuary is a major fish spawning and nursery area, and home to important birds, fish and plants as well as three types of turtles: the green, loggerhead, and hoax. It's bird of Prey Center, the first of its kind in the Middle East, is home to 50 different types of birds of prey, including 14 permanently settled species along the Eastern Coast. Seer Bu Neer Island is a historical, cultural, and environmental landmark that is rich in coral reefs, immigrating birds and green turtles, Wadi Al Helow is rich in reptiles, rodents, birds, and fresh water fishes and Wasit is rich in birds, reptiles and saline plants. Protected areas in the Central region, including Al Doulaimah, Al Bardy and Al Fayah are known for their stone plains, Samar and Ghaf Trees.

Sir Bu Nuair Island
SIR BU NUAIR ISLAND was announced as nature reserve on 10, December 2000. Stretching over an area of 13 square kilometers, the uninhabited pearl-shaped Island is located 65 km away from the coast of the United Arab Emirates on the Arabian Gulf. A trip to the island takes between 2-3 hours by sea, and 40 minutes by air from Sharjah. SIR BU NUAIR certainly deserves its recognition as a wetland of international importance because of its important environmental

features, including geological layers, natural plants and seabirds, as well as beautiful scenery.

Progress has been made on listing SIR BU NUAIR ISLAND, a global heritage site by UNESCO, as the island constitutes a natural refuge for turtles for more than 2,000 years, and known for its vibrant marine environment. Studies of marine surveys, made on the island, revealed that there are approximately twenty different types of coral reefs, including Brain corals, the Bee Hive, the Dendritic, Deer Horns, and others, and 58 reef fish species have been recorded during surveys conducted in northern and western reefs areas in SIR BU NUAIR Island.

It is worth mentioning that the development of SIR BU NUAIR project is considered one of the most important and largest "Shurooq" initiatives, in order to make the island a destination like no other. The island will feature a spa, a five-star hotel, villas and hotel apartments, along with a number of shops, restaurants and other leisure facilities. SIR BU NUAIR ISLAND contributes to promoting the modern lifestyle which combines the beauty of the region and its cultural heritage through the unique architectural design of the island facilities and through the hospitality deals provided by to the visitors.

Scheduled to be completed on 2017, SIR BU NUAIR project will feature a village for camping, theater, museum, mosque, education center, sea port and airport. The island also seeks to follow the vital social and commercial life offered in cities and small ports around the world.

Khor Kalba Nature Reserve

Stretching over 1230 hectares, Khor Kalba nature reserve is one of the oldest and largest green natural sites on the East |Coast of the UAE.

It is a shelter for many endangered birds such as Egret and Halcyon.

This beautiful and quiet area filled with green plants and trees constitutes a great backdrop for large rocks and steep cliffs of the Al Hajar (stone) mountains.

Wadi Al Helow Protected Area

Wadi Al Helow

Located on the road from Sharjah to Kalba, it was declared as a nature reserve in 2007. It aims to protect the valleys and mountain environment and the preservation of the physical and biological resources such as birds, reptiles, rodents and freshwater fish

Wasit Nature Reserve

Located in Al Ramtha area, It was declared as a nature reserve in 2007, what makes this nature reverse unique is the environmental diversity of coastal sand dunes, salt and debris linking ponds and large open lake with the island. It has 198 different species of birds, besides the great diversity in the species of small mammals, reptiles and insects, discovered for the first time in the UAE.

Al Doulaimah Nature Reserve

Located on the road from Sharjah to Al Dhaid, and specifically to the east of the intersection no. 12, the name Al Doulaimah is referring to the darkness of this place even in the day time, due to the lush of trees which was covering the entire area.

Tigers, antelopes, wolves, rabbits, deer, foxes, some reptiles and locusts, in addition to the birds, were living there.

It Was declared as nature reserve in 2007, based on the directions of His Highness Sheikh Dr. Sultan bin Mohammed Al Qasimi, Supreme Council Member and Ruler of Sharjah, in order to rescue those species from the case of significant deterioration caused by drought and hunting; after that the area was fenced and several wild animals were released, a large group of trees were planted, and wells were set, to provide an appropriate atmosphere for plants and animals, which turned it into one of the most important nature reserves in Sharjah.

Jabal Al Fayah Reserve
The geographical location of this nature reserve, within a prominent archaeological site in Sharjah, has made it one of the significant protected areas in Sharjah. It was declared as a nature reserve in 2007 in order to protect the geological structures, the archaeological areas, and the physical resources.

Al Madina Nature Reserve
It is one of the oldest nature reserves in Sharjah, it was announced in 1996, located in the central region of Maliha on the road from Sharjah to Kalba. This nature reserve was designed to protect the ecosystem

of the gravel plains, the physical resources, and trees in the region, as well as a variety of species of birds and reptiles.

Al Hefya Nature Reserve
Stretching from Wadi Al Helou area up to Khor Kalba sea overlooking the coast of Oman. This nature reserve constitutes a fertile environment for the production of good quality honey. Moreover it includes a beautiful protected species of birds that nest and lay eggs in this region such as wild pigeons and Hoopoe, hawks and many other species of birds. This area was designed to protect the environment of flood plains adjacent to the foothills of the mountains, which is a safe haven for rare species of animals and birds.

Ras Al Khaimah

Ras Al Khaimah is located on the coast of the Arabian Gulf with a length of about 64 km and more than 128 kilometers deep inside the land. Ras Al Khaimah shares mountainous borders with the Sultanate of Oman from the South and the North-East side. Many islands in the Arabian Gulf belong to the Emirate of Ras Al Khaimah, the most important among them are the Greater Tamb Island and the Lesser Tamb Island. The area of Ras Al Khaimah is about 1684 square kilometers, which is equivalent to 2.2% of the total area of the country, without the Islands belonging to it. The total population of Ras Al Khaimah is around 250,000 people according to the census of December 2005.

The City of Ras Al Khaimah is the capital of the Emirate and it is divided into two parts by the Creek of Khor Ras Al Khaimah. The Western part of Ras Al Khaimah is known as the Old Town, where the National Museum of Ras Al Khaimah and some government departments are located ; the Eastern part of Ras Al Khaimah, which is known as AL Nakheel, includes the residence of His Highness Sheikh Saud bin Saqr Al Qasmi, as well as some government departments and businesses centers. The two parts of Ras Al Khaimah are connected by a major bridge going over the creek to facilitate the traffic movement.

One of the major industrial areas of Ras Al Khaiman is Khor Khwair, which is located 25 kilometers to the North, it is famous for many important industries such as cement, stone and marble manufactories. Another important area in Khor Khwair is Sheikh Saqr Port.

Ras Al Khaimah is rich with the traditional remains of the great Julfar City, Forts and Valleys. It is also famous for its unique location : mountains, coasts and regions of agricultural and natural hot springs such as the resort of Ain Khatt, which is frequently visited by many tourists and people, who seek some kinds of health treatment.

Attractions & nightlife

City break in Ras al Khaimah. Active leisure ideas for Ras al Khaimah - attractions, recreation and nightlife

Ras Al Khaimah has a perfect entertainment infrastructure. Here, you can find everything for proper and diverse pastime: amazing water parks, shopping and entertainment centers, vast markets, a lot of restaurants, pubs and picturesque nightclubs.

TheIceland Water Park opened in 2010 and being the largest in the United Arab Emirates is located exactly here. The main peculiarity of the water park is its unusual design: it is decorated as a classical arctic scene. The recreation area is decorated with models of glaciers and snow-white drifts, as well as of penguins making the atmosphere even more realistic. The main gem of the water park is a huge artificial waterfall, which height is 37 m. Visitors of the center can try a lot of exciting attractions, slides and other extreme entertainments.

You can get away of the hot sun in the shopping and entertainment Al Manar Mall that has long been a place where interesting cultural events are held. Shopping enthusiasts can visit hundreds of boutiques that will certainly surprise with their prices. An excellent playing area is equipped for the little guests. In the shopping mall, there are wonderful cafes, restaurants and a large showroom.

Elite sports fans are recommended to visit the best golf club in the emirate - Al Hamra Golf Club. The whole family can comfortably relax here. Professional trainers are ready to offer beginners their services. Remarkably, they can teach not only adults, but also children from 4 years of age how to play golf. Professional sportsmen will not be bored too, as they will certainly be pleased with a high quality of training areas. On the territory of the club, attractive restaurants and cafes work and beautiful recreation areas are equipped for vacationers' convenience.

As for shopping, the popular Safeer Mall Shopping Center should be noted. It occupies a very spectacular building in national style and attracts clients with affordable prices. The shopping center includes more than a hundred shops of different specialization. The considerable part of the mall is occupied by a children's entertainment center with many exciting attractions. Visitors can recover after riding and shopping in one of the comfortable restaurants.

Those travelers who are going to bring elite alcohol from abroad should certainly drop in a special shop called Power House. Here, prices of alcoholic products are the lowest in the emirate and the quality is always high. In the evening, active tourists can walk along the coastline. There are the largest hotels and the noisiest and most popular nightclubs.

They include the White pub located in the vicinity of the Al Hamra Palace hotel. In the evenings, very interesting entertainments are organized in the pub. Its visitors have an opportunity not only to taste exquisite cocktails, but also to order specialties in the nearby restaurant. The popular pub Coconut Grove located near the hotel Bin

Majid Resort Ras Al Khaimah and having a great choice of treats will certainly please fans of recreation in a romantic atmosphere.

Guide to Ras al Khaimah

Sightseeing in Ras al Khaimah what to see. Complete travel guide

Ras al-Khaimah, the most northern and smallest emirate, is a tourist center of global significance. It has many unique features, due to which it has gained fame and popularity. Nowadays, the picturesque emirate attracts admirers of very different kinds of recreation. The variety of landscapes situated on the territory of 1 700 square meters should be primarily noted. There are large desert areas that are so typical for the United Arab Emirates, as well as green oases buried in exotic plants and being a location of the most popular resorts.

Today, fertile lands are covered with spacious plantations. Visitors of the emirate have an opportunity to walk along picturesque orchards. Of particular interest for vacationers is a coastal zone of the emirate. The total length of beaches of Ras al-Khaimah is more than 60 kilometers. Almost all plots of the coast are built up with large hotels. The coastline of the emirate is a single extensive resort and entertainment center.

Taking into account the diversity of landscapes described above, different kinds of recreation are available for guests of the picturesque emirate. There, you can peacefully relax at the coast or do a positive introduction to scuba diving, go for a walk along the desert or take a closer look at flora and fauna in one of the tropical forests, enjoy natural splendor far from noisy resort districts or immerse into the bustle of lively streets.

Known historically as a prosperous trade center, the emirate was located at the crossroads of significant trade routes. The first settlements in the area, where the emirate is located now, appeared in the prehistoric period, what is evidenced by multiple archaeological finds. For travelers, the region is interesting not only due to its first-class beach hotels and nature attractions, but also multiple great markets and shopping centers. Admirers of excursion tourism will be impressed with a diversity of historical sites and unique archaeological expeditions.

One of the main symbols of the emirate is healing thermal springs called Khatt. Within the area around springs there is an upscale wellness center that attracts guests from all over the world. The Khatt district is famous for its picturesque landscapes and relaxing atmosphere. This resort area is popular with older people and tourists who prefer calm recreation.

Shopping admirers are more interested in the center district of the emirate where they can visit amazing markets and shopping malls. The supermarket called Carrefour is at the peak of popularity. It still remains the oldest shop in Ras al-Khaimah, as there you can buy absolutely everything you want. Also, the diversity of culinary venues should be noted. In the emirate, there are different culinary directions. Small street cafes and outdoor stands where you can buy cheap and interesting treats, such as pizza, kebab and pastry, are quite popular with most of tourists.

Over the past decades, the tourist infrastructure of the emirate has significantly changed. Today, this is a location of upscale resort hotels. Travelers can visit fully equipped beaches, excellent water parks and many other venues where they can enjoy wonderful family recreation. This is important to take into account that Ras al-Khaimah is one of the free emirates in terms of local laws and rules, so foreign guests won't feel uneasy and confused.

Andorra la Vella is a comfortable resort that is perfectly suitable for a family vacation. Tourists with children will be genuinely pleased with the variety of entertainment options available to them. Consider visiting Naturlandia – this popular entertainment center is located in the neighborhood of the resort. Vacationers can enjoy all of the amusements in warm months. There are playgrounds and various amusements for children of different age and for adults. Assault courses at Naturlandia are particularly popular with visitors. Small children will enjoy a visit to a small zoo that is also open in the territory of the complex. This zoo has only friendly animals that children can pet and feed.

The nearby town of Canillo is home to another place that deserves a visit, Palau de Gel. It takes only 20 minutes to reach the ice palace from the capital. The complex offers a rich choice of entertainments for the whole family. Besides a traditional ice skating rink, there are ice quests, and even carting. Those who have always dreamt of learning how to ice skate will also find it very interesting to visit this center. There is a rental office that has quality sports gear. Once you have the necessary equipment, simply hire a professional instructor who will teach you how to skate.

When it is getting dark, numerous guests of the resort head to Placa del Poble. The district formed around this square is rich in entertainment. There are a concert hall, a theater, several shopping centers, numerous interesting shops, and, of course, numerous restaurants and bars. It is no less interesting to visit this district in the daytime because many souvenir shops and outlets tend to close quite early.

Culture: sights to visit

Culture of Ras al Khaimah. Places to visit - old town, temples, theaters, museums and palaces

Tour enthusiasts who choose Ras al-Khaimah for their recreation have an opportunity to visit a lot of interesting natural and historical attractions. On the territory of the emirate, there is the Canyon of Hadzharsky Mountains that resembles a huge oasis surrounded by desert landscapes. In the canyon, stones that are subsequently used for the modern building construction in the most popular UAE resort areas are extracted. The canyon attracts travelers with a diversity of its plants. When walking here, you can see a lot of rare animals, birds and insects.

No doubt, the most visited cultural center is the Ras Al Khaimah Museum located in the incomparably beautiful Fort Al Husen. The fort was built in the 18th century and remained a permanent residence of the royal family till 1964. In 1987, under Sheikh Saqr bin Moḥammad Al Qasimi, the historical construction started being used as a large museum. Nowadays, a rich collection of archaeological finds and ethnological exhibits is kept in the fort. Visitors of the museum can see ancient manuscripts, unique historical documents, collections of old weapons and archeologists' finds that were found directly on the territory of the emirate.

There are a lot of modern architectural constructions among interesting attractions, including the City bridge in Ras Al Khaimah. The bridge runs above the bay and connects old and new parts of the emirate. It is possible to cross it not only by car, but also on foot.

Convenient and safe trails are equipped for pedestrians. The bridge has a spectacular panoramic view of the bay and coastal areas of Ras Al Khaimah. The bridge is a part of the lively Al-Hisn Rd that is a location of popular hotels, restaurants, shops and different entertainment centers.

Those who like walking along historical places should visit the district of Khatt. There are important historical objects, the North and South Watch Towers. In the late 19th century, they protected the small settlement of Khatt from invaders. Towers have managed to survive to this day. They are located on a small hill. All towers have wonderful viewing platforms.

One of the unusual and attractive cultural sites is the Museum and the center of Ahmed bin Majid called after the great navigator. Exhibits of the museum are dedicated to discoveries of the great traveler and to the history of the fishery development. Exhibits of the museum include old devices used by pearl catchers and local anglers hundreds of years ago. Some of the most original exhibits of the museum are old boats. Art connoisseurs will be definitely impressed by incredible paintings made of fine shells.

The real trove of historical attractions is a picturesque district of Khatt. Besides ancient towers, you can see here a lot of interesting sites. Exactly here, archeologists found ancient tombs and a great number of other unique exhibits that are represented in the largest museum of the emirate today. Now Khatt is an agricultural center of the emirate where lively streets interchange with vast date and fruit plantations.

In the section below, you can get one of our excursion tickets or city discovery tours over Ras al Khaimah and surroundings. Our website offers 10-30% lower ticket prices, when compared to the offline purchase on the spot.

Ajman

The Emirate of Ajman is located on the Arabian Gulf, with a coast length of about 16 Kilometers, between the Emirates of Sharjah and Umm Al Quwain. The Emirate covers an area of about 259 square kilometers, equivalent to 0.3% of the total area of the country, without counting its islands. It has a population of 206,997 according to the census of December 2005. Ajman City, the capital of the Emirate of Ajman, is located on the coast of the Arabian Gulf. Ajman City is also the residence of His Highness Sheikh Humaid Bin Rashid al Nuaimi, the Ruler. It accommodates all the government departments, companies, banks, commercial markets and the port of Ajman, which is located on the Creek, that passes through the city.

Although Ajman has become a modern city, that provides modern services and facilities, it has maintained its old traditional character, which enables the Emirate to occupy a privileged position, that combines the achievements of the modern age with the authenticity of the ancient past. The charming beaches of Ajman provide fresh air, far away from noise and pollution. They attract many sea lovers to do different activities.

Masfout is one of the famous areas in the South-East of the Emirate of Ajman. It is about 110 km away from the city. Masfout is famous for agriculture, fertile soil spacious valleys and moderate climate, which made it a center for tourists and tourism. Masfout has a marvelous picturesque nature, that gives the surrounding mountains in the area a breathtaking beauty.

The Fort of Ajman is a highlighted monument in the country, dating back to the eighteenth century. It conveys the reality of life in different eras. The fort was renovated and converted into a museum containing integrated models of antiquities, traditional artifacts and pictures of ancient social life.

Ajman Attraction

The area of Ajman emirate is about 460sq. Km. while the total area including the international waters is about 600 sqs. Km. & the coastal part of Ajman Emirate of 16 Km. long located on the coast of the Gulf. Ajman Emirates is formed of three geographical regions which are afar of each other & topographically different according to its distance from the coast of the Gulf. These regions are Ajman city, Masfout region & Al Manama region.

The climate of the Emirate in general is moderate as the temperature & the humidity is high in summer, & winter the temperature may reach 25 Degree Celcius..

There are plenty of promises for tourists and tourism in Ajman owing to its varied features of its economic development, currently prevailing in the Emirates. Tourist attractions are represented by the golden sandy beaches and different natural topography lying between mountains and flat sand. And to rop it is the precious historical treasures of Ajman museum containing a host of exhibits displayed in a scientific and charming way.

Due to the Directives of His Highness, Ruler of Ajman, the municipality of Ajman makes considerable efforts to complete the infrastructure construction of the tourism industry by improving and developing the sea-side by making spacious cars parks, pedestrian passage and opening new entertainment centers.

The Ajman National Museum represents one of the main tourist attractions in the City. It is also one of the most important historical forts and fortresses spread all over the country related to the early history of the Emirates. The Museum can be considered with its content of different civilization inheritances which represent the historical year of the Emirate in particular and the area in general, as a center to know the ways of living in the past through the archeological acquisitions, the historical documents and tools which were used during those days as the means of life. The archeological discoveries which happened in the past year prove that Ajman knew the human settlement on its land more than five thousand year ago.

The Belgian delegation of Legant University has found many important discoveries in the area of Muaihat, Al Zawara and Masfout going back to the period 2500 & 3500 B.C. In these discoveries many tools, hand made articles, jewelerly and vessels with different shapes for different purposes were found which indicates these area may have been considered as first civilized human settlements in the past. These archeological discoveries all around the Emirates show that the area had good trading relations with the civilization of Delmon, Jamrat Nasr and Loristion in west, east and south of the gulf, and the civilization of Mohenjodaro in the Sindh valley, India and far East.

The construction boom in Ajman is continuing and improving the infrastructure facilities is in progress. During 1999 and 2000 many high-rise residential and commercial building were constructed, reflecting distinguished architectural designs.

In light of the considerable developments which is witnessed by the Minicipality & Planning Dept. in Ajman, entered GIS (Geographic information systems) which is a computer-based tool mapping & analyzing things that exist on earth.

GIS links information (attributes) to location data (Maps) This link allows us to layer that information to get a better understanding of how it all works together. These abilities distinguish GIS from other information systems and make it valuable to a wide range of public and private establishments in Ajman Emirate. The ability of GIS to search multiple databases and perform complex geographic queries provides significant time and cost savings.

Al Manama Region

It is situated on a leveled land full with rough pebbles & there are some spots of agricultural land available in this region like Munsat Valley, al Safsaf & Boay al Nakhil valley which is located between Ashqar mountain & Ben Alwah Mountain. It's about 60 km. to the east of Ajman city where there is an adjacent road to the region which is also the main road going to Fujairah through Sharjah.

Masfout Region

It is about 130 km. far from Ajman to eastern south & includes Sasfout city, Mzairea & Sabeigah towns. The inhabitants descend from the tribes known as Bodawat & Bany Kaab deeply rooted in the area. The area is composed of fascinating scenery mainly calcium stone mountains extending to the Sultanate of Oman. Across these mountains there are valleys with high fertile arable soil & running water during winter as well as summer. There are valleys like Leshn, Gulfa, Leem, Defdhaa, Al Khanfareyah, Al Swamer & Hadf valley.

Because of these valleys the area is considered to be an agricultural area in the region.

Ajman Fort

The fort is believed to have been built in the late eighteenth century. Local materials such as coral stones of the sea and gypsum were used in building this Fort, special tree trunks brought from East Africa were used for its ceiling. In 1820 the Fort, like all other citadels and forts in the Northern Emirates, was shelled by the British war ships. The Fort was destroyed but it was rebuilt by Sheikh Rashid Bin Humaid I (1803-1838).

During the nineteenth and twentieth centuries the Fort witnessed restoration and addition processes. It remained as residence place of the Ruling Family until the year 1970 when H.H. the late Sheikh Rashid Bin Humaid Al Nuaim (1920-1981) moved to live in Al Zaher Palace and the Fort became the headquarters of Ajman Police during the period (1970-1981). In the late 1980s H.H. Sheikh Humaid Bin Rashid Al Nuaimi, Member of the Supreme Council, Ruler of Ajman, gave his directives to restore the Fort in order to change it in to a museum for Emirates heritage. The restoration process, which was under the supervision of a group of experts, lasted for three years.

Description of the Fort

After World War II, Mr. Remond Aushia, the agent of the British Airways in Sharjah, visited the fort and wrote a detailed article describing the fort in his book "kings of sands". That visit came as a result of an invitation extended to him by the Ruler of Ajman, the late Sheikh Rashid Bin Humaid Al Nuaimi. The article was wntitled "A Fishing Trip in the Hospitable Reception of Sheikh Rashid Bin Humaid". He said in his article: "The Palace is a great building which attracts attention. There is a huge arch built on two stands on top of its large gate.

All these were made of dark honey-coloured sand stones. It is one of the most beautiful citadels in Ajman. It is supported by high towers which look like the crusade Citadels in the wall of AKKA in Palestine. Two of these tower were in a direction towards the south. The architecture of the palace was common in the seventeenth century. They looked like battlements because of the unstable conditions of war which prevailed in the desert during that period. The people of Ajman are well known for their heroism throughout the whole region and they are true warriors.

Sightseeing

Ajman's location within a short flight's distance from key markets in Europe and Asia, combined with its beautiful beaches, solid transport infrastructure and a warm and welcoming culture, make the emirate an ideal vacation spot. With busier and more crowded emirates adjacent, Ajman has become a place for vacationers to get away from it all with many luxurious hotel offerings. A number of five-star hotels are slated for completion along the Ajman corniche and elsewhere around the city. Another project, aimed at people looking for something with a more natural feel, the Al Zohra project on the eastern side of Ajman Creek, will provide an exclusive, integrated vacation and residential destination. Ajman overall has a luxurious, serene, peaceful and yet exclusive feel.

The Ajman museum

The Ajman Museum is housed in an 18th C fortress that was used as a stronghold for the Emirates leadership and as a first line of defense. The fort was the ruler's palace and then the Ajman police station. Two wind towers and two watch towers were maintained when the fort was renovated. A large gate and two cannons are located on the front of the fort.

Dhow Yard

This sightseeing attraction is a must-see for tourists visiting Ajman, as this is regarded as the world's largest, still active boat building yard and it is also the largest dhow building yard in the emirates. To give background, the term dhow defines: a traditional boat of Arabian origin with one or more lateen sails. Earlier it was used in vogue in trade as well as for war and other maritime purposes. The dhows which were larger in size had about 30 crews and the smaller ones had around 12 crews. The Dhows are ocean-going vessels and they are built using the traditional tools with the manual skills that are not written down in any blueprint but has been handed down from generations. The dhows of Ajman are regarded as the best in quality among the Emirates and the dhow yard is certainly worth a visit as sightseers can witness a dhow being built right before their eyes.

Mowaihat

Mowaihat is one of the most famous archaeological sites of the entire United Arab Emirates. At the time of its discovery (in 1986 while new sewage pipe was being laid), the municipal workers discovered a circular tomb which was the style of the Umm al-Nar period. This tomb dates back to 2000 to 2500 BC and is 8.25M in diameter. After the conduction of the excavation, various artifacts were from the site including: soft stones and painted ceramic vessels from the Umm al-Nar period, along with beads, two stamp seals and a number of copper implements. The material form this excavation site forms the bulk of the archaeological artifacts on display in the Ajman museum

Economy of Ajman

The Ajman economy has been largely dependent on fishing and trade. However, the trend of general economic development in the UAE has caught up with Ajman, too. The emirate has drawn several commercial and industrial enterprises, given, its proximity to commercial centres of Dubai and Sharjah, and its comparatively low rentals. The prominent additions to the Ajman economy recently are the Free Zone, resort hotels, Ajman City Centre shopping complex, and a host of educational institutions.

Ajman has witnessed rapid growth recently, with several construction projects being implemented. Ajman has established itself as a major business centre, drawing investors - both local and international.

Population of Ajman

The population of Ajman is 262,186 towards end of 2011, said statistics from Ajman Executive Council Show. Expatriates account for more than 80percent of total population. Ajman is the fifth largest emirate in the UAE in terms of GDP and population. The largest is Abu Dhabi, followed by Dubai, Sharjah, and Ras Al Khaimah.

Major attractions in Ajman

Ajman holds plenty of promises to tourists, owing to varied features of economic development currently prevailing in the emirates. Ajman is witnessing considerable growth and development, just like in the rest of the UAE, and therefore, tourist attractions and activities, including shopping, cultural and shopping opportunities are growing rapidly.

Ajman National Museum

Built in the late 18th century, this was one of the main tourist attractions in the city, and one of the most historical forts spread across the country. The Museum, which was once a Ruler's palace, could be the right place to view the inheritances of various civilizations, representing the history of the emirate, and the area in general. Various ways of living in the past can be known through archeological acquisitions, historical documents and tools that were in use during the past.

Ajman Fort

The Ajman Fort, believed to be built in the late 18th century, but, was shelled by the British war ships in 1820. It was built with local materials such as coral stones of the sea and gypsum, while special tree trunks brought from East Africa has been used for the ceiling. Later, the Fort was restored during the 19th and 20th centuries. It was the residence of the Ruling families in the past. There is a huge arch built on two stands on top of its large gates, made of honey-coloured sandstones. It has been described as one of the most beautiful citadels in Ajman.

Sheikh Zayed Ajman Mosque

There are several religious sites in Ajman, the most prominent of them being the Sheikh Zayed Ajman Mosque. The rich architecture of the Mosque is impressive. The Mosque is said to have been built for Late Sheikh Rashid bin Humaid Al Nuaimi, by his son and current Ruler of

Ajman, Humaid bin Rashid Al Nuaimi. The Mosque is a major landmark in Ajman City.

Etisalat Tower
Ajman has experienced major construction boom in recent years. The gleaming new Etisalat Tower seems like an instant landmark within Ajman City. The tower is designed in traditional Mosque-style. The tower is topped by a large sphere, referred to as 'giant golf ball'. The tower is one of the world's most distinctive skyscrapers.

The Emirates City
This is one of the popular projects in Ajman. Emirates City is a residential and commercial development (almost the size of a small town), built in the emirate of Ajman. The Dh.15bn worth freehold development, located on the Emirates Road, began as a small project, but, now has more than hundred buildings, several shopping malls and best hotels. It is located in proximity to Al Ameera Village, and is just 20 minutes away from Dubai and Sharjah International Airports.

The towers in the Emirates City is located amidst lakes and green parks, and comprises Mosques, Shopping Districts, five-star restaurants, educational and medical amenities.

Dhow Yard
Tourists in Ajman have always enjoyed visit to Dhow Yard. Here, visitors get to see the dhows being built in a traditional manner. There are also modern speed boats being built here, to compete in the Dubai

Speed Boat Races. The Ajman Dhow Yard is the world's largest boat building yard, and the biggest dhow building centre. Located along the northern end of the creek, it can house more than 30 boats at a time. Several of these are built with fiber glass, rather than wood.

Beaches
The beaches in Ajman have always been the traditional tourist attraction spots, as the climate of Ajman is apt for beach life. The dolphins are common off the coast of Ajman, and dolphin spotting is a popular recreation with tourists and locals alike.

Shopping/dining
Shopping is a popular activity in Ajman, as there are both, the modern malls with designer and luxury items, offering all commodities, otherwise available in the shopping malls elsewhere in the UAE, and there are the traditional shops selling local products too.

Ajman also has various eateries ranging from western fast food outlets, to high-class restaurants and traditional cafe and street vendors. Although Ajman is a Muslim state, alcohol can be purchased in hotels and restaurants too. This is the norm in the UAE.

Umm Al Quwain
The Emirate Umm Al Quwain is located on the coast of the Arabian Gulf and its territory stretches on about 24 kilometers along the coast between the Emirates of Sharjah (west) and Ras Al Khaimah (east).

The area of Umm Al Quwain is approximately 777 square kilometers, which is equivalent to 1 % of the total area of the country (its islands excluded). The Population of the Emirate of Umm Al Quwain is 49159 according to the census of December 2005. The city of Umm Al Quwain is the capital of the Emirate.

The population, of the Emirate of Umm Al Quwain, is 49 159 people, according to the census of December 2005. The city of Umm Al Quwain is the capital of the Emirate. There is a deep Creek in the city with a length of about five kilometers and a width of one kilometer. The city is the residence of His Highness Sheikh Saud bin Rashid Al Mualla. It also hosts all government departments, companies, banks, commercial markets, commercial seaport and the Marine Research Center, that helps in the development of fisheries in the country.

One of the Emirate suburbs is the city of Falaj Al Mualla, which is located 50 kilometers south -east of Umm Al Quwain. The name comes from the "Falaj" which is the water, that comes out of the ground or from the mountains. The vast spread of agriculture in Falaj Al Mualla is due to the fertility of the soil and the availability of fresh water.

Siniya Island is about 1 km from the city of Umm Al Quwain, and extends on an area of about 90 square kilometers. It is a natural reserve for deer, sea birds and mangroves. The remains along the coast, near Umm Al Quwain, reveal the oldest archeological city that was flourishing more than two thousand years ago in the south east of the Arabian Peninsula, which is called Al Dour. Excavations conducted by archaeologists show many archaeological findings such as ancient stone homes, stone graves, ceramics, Egyptian and Shami (Mesopotamian) glass tools

Attractions and Activities in Umm al Quwain

Umm Al Quwain may be only 40 miles from Dubai, but it is a world apart in atmosphere. Quieter and slightly less developed than Dubai, this small emirate has a beautiful sandy beach and plenty of traditional Arabian activities as well as modern family-friendly attractions and things to do.

Cultural Activities Around Umm Al Quwain
Camel Racing is a popular sport in the UAE and there is a race track at Al Labsa. Spectators are welcome to watch the thrilling races on Thursdays and Fridays in the cooler months. You may also spot camel caravans moving across the dunes as the camels are moved between race tracks.

The high sand dunes around the city of Umm al Quwain are ideal for off-road vehicles and quad bikes. Known as dune-bashing, this exhilarating experience provides a unique desert activity.

Take a trip to one of the islands in the creek. Al Sinnayah is the largest of these uninhabited islands which are an unprotected nature reserve for water birds, nesting cormorants and Arabian gazelle.

Historic Attractions Around Umm Al Quwain

Visit the old port area and see the fishing fleet and dhow boat builders who still make these simple wooden sail boats by hand.

Historic Umm Al Quwain Fort is a grand restored fortress with an impressive entrance. Once the home of the ruling sheikh and later used as a prison, it now is a museum filled with artefacts, weapons, jewellery and pottery unearthed in the region.

Family Friendly Attractions Around Umm Al Quwain

The top attraction for families has to be the Dreamland Aqua Park. Said to be the largest water park in the world, this oasis of palm trees and water-themed activities is a wonderful place to cool off on a hot day in the desert.

As well as a family raft ride and wave pool there is a high salinity pool for floating effortlessly, watersports, lazy river, aqua play, volleyball and an enormous Jacuzzi. Rides include the Black Hole, Twisting Dragons, Kamikaze, Space Bowl and Roaring Volcano, along with five giant water slides. Best of all the admission is all-inclusive so you can enjoy all the rides and pools for once great price (around AED 129 or

£23). Dry off and enjoy a meal in one of the seven international restaurants or challenge the family in the video games arcade.

Swimming and snorkelling are popular right off the beach in Umm al Quwain, but if you don't want to get your hair wet you can see plenty of marine life, rays, sharks and corals at the Aquarium and Marine Science Centre. Located beside the new port, the Marine Research Centre may require advanced booking.

Happyland is another local theme park with video games, bouncy castles and other kid's activities. Suitable for all ages, this park offers plenty of opportunity for youngsters to run around and have fun.

Of course, the biggest attraction for visitors to Umm al Quwain has to be the beach where visitors can enjoy swimming, sunbathing, snorkelling, sailing, jet skiing and waterskiing. Have fun!

Things to do in Umm Al Quwain

It is said that Umm Al Quwain (UAQ) is the best place in the world for people who enjoy sounds of waves and peace. Sailing in the calm water of lagoon offers best and most interesting sailing in the Northern Emirates.

Water-skiing
UAQ is ideal for water-skiing, kayaking, wind-surfing and jet-skiing. The adventurous visitors could actually sail and canoe through the clear, calm waters to deserted islands and explore the mangrove swamps,

wherein dwells several seabirds, insects and fish. There are also pink flamingos, turtles, crabs and jumping fish in the natural environment.

UAQ Marine Club and Riding Center

Located not far from fish souq is a large stretch of shaded beach facing the lagoon. Established in 1979, the riding club has more than 40 horses and a team of qualified riding instructors.

UAQ Aeroclub

Located not far from Dreamland is the UAE aviation club, set up under the patronage of Sheikh Mohammed Bin Rashid Al Mualla. The club is renowned for its skydiving and parachute championships. It also offers opportunities for flying, hot air ballooning, parachuting, skydiving (both single and tandem) and paramonting in the UAE. Training is also offered throughout the year.

UAQ Motor Racing Club

Located along the city side of Dreamland, it offers visitors the opportunity to experience the speed, exhilaration and thrill of off-road dune motor hiking, buggy racing in three purpose-built arenas.

Falaj Al Mualla Garden Park

Located a couple of meters away from UAQ bridge, is the emirates road or outer bypass road. It offers several facilities including swimming pools for adults and kids, apart from kids playground, bbq areas, mini grocery, bikes rental, and tricycle ride.

Bird watching

Bird watchers can enjoy wonderful wildlife at Khor al Beidah and other popular sights lying to south and east of the town. The Al Sinniyah Island, a marine sanctuary covering 90sqkms, and the largest of all islands, is also visible from the Corniche. During the period November to March several great cormorants and other seabirds, are spotted regularly flying few feet above the sea. Shallow lagoons and mud flats get together to combine and create the perfect habitats for feeding and nesting for several species of heron and plover, apart from flamingos, gulls and terns.

Dhow building, Camel racing, fishing, falconry
Dhow building, fishing, camel racing and falconry are few popular sports in UAQ. The craftsmen continue to build traditional boats in the dhow building yard. Shahin or peregrine falcons can be seen in the region, apart from the Al-Hur light-skinned hunting hawk.

The camel race track at Al Labsa offers an exceptionally pretty drive. It is set up in the lee of large dunes, located to left of road leading to Falaj Al Moalla. Camel caravans are a familiar site here, crossing the desert from one race track to another. The dunes in this area, combined with wooded dales, offer a challenging terrain for off road desert drivers and they are referred to as "dune bashers".

Palma Bowling

The palma bowling is more than bowling. There is pool (snooker), video games, shisha bar, beachside restaurant, and more. The place gives a feel of Egypt and could easily be reached through taxi.

Umm Al Quwain Tourist Spots:
UAQ Museum
The UAQ Museum is a renovated ancient fort used to guard entrance to the old town. The museum houses several artifacts found near archeological sites. Another excavated site, Al-Dur, was actually a coastal city with nearly 200 BCE until the third century CE. The site also contains several interesting artifacts that are housed in the UAQ Museum.

Dreamland
Dreamland is one of the major tourist attractions and is the largest water park in the UAE. Covering about 250,000 square meters, the park features high-salinity pool, raft rides, wave pool, swimming pool, lazy river, several water slides, spa-like pool with a bar for relaxing. Dreamland is just an hour and a half drive from Dubai.

Aquarium
It is on the headland beside the new port. Being a part of Marine Research Centre, it is open to visitors by prior appointment. It features several fish and sea life found in the region, including snakes and corals and rays.

Happyland

It is a kids' haven with attractive video games, jumping castles and all other entertainment for kids.

UAQ Islands
They lie to the east of mainland peninsula on a unique stretch of coastline comprising sandy islands surrounded by thick mangrove forests separated by series of creeks. The largest among seven islands is Al Sinniyah, followed by Jazirat Al Ghallah and Al Keabe, all visible from old towns. In between these, there is the coastal plains and smaller islands of Al Qaram, Al Sow, Al Harmala and Al Chewria. The Madaar creek running between the islands offer a navigable waterway for fisherman even at low tide when average depth is less than few feet.

Other amenities:
Umm Al Quwain also has great shops like the Lulu Hypermarket offering garments, grocery, foodstuffs, perfumes and electronics, the Salma Market – although small is known for cheap clothes, Al Manamah Hypermarket – is good to shop and offers garments, groceries, foodstuff and perfumes and electronics.

As for eateries, the Al-Ramlah Cafetaria, KFC, Arabian Chicken Hut, Wadi Al Neel Seafood restaurant, baskin robbins, cardoba restaurant, Sadaf cafeteria, and Al Foren Al Sakhen Pastries and Pies are all good choices.

Few good options for accommodation are Umm Al Quwain Beach Hotel, Barracuda Beach Resort (offers beach, swimming pool, bbq grills and duty-free liquor store, Flamingo Beach Resort (great place for beach vacationers, offers water sports, diving, snorkelling, fishing, crab hunting, glass bottom boat rides), Pearl Hotel, Palma Beach Hotel, Barracuda Beach Resort, and Royal Residence Resort Villas.

The End

www.ingramcontent.com/pod-product-compliance
Lightning Source LLC
Chambersburg PA
CBHW021434080526
44588CB00009B/524